# BIBLIOGRAPHY OF RESEARCH PROJECTS REPORTS

CHECK LIST OF HISTORICAL RECORDS SURVEY PUBLICATIONS

W. P. A. Technical Series
Research and Records Bibliography No. 7

Revised April, 1943

FEDERAL WORKS AGENCY
WORK PROJECTS ADMINISTRATION
Division of Service Projects
Washington, D. C.

> *Notice*
>
> This book has been reproduced from an original mimeographed edition of an original transcription of records by the Work Progress Administration (WPA) in 1930s or 1940s.. In many instances, the resulting text is light, the documents are physically flawed, and foxing (or discoloration) occurs. The pages of this reprint have been digitally enhanced and, where possible, the flaws eliminated in order to provide clarity of content and a pleasant reading experience.

*Bibliography of Research Projects Reports: Check List of Historical Records Survey Publications*

Originally transcribed by:

The Work Progress Administration (WPA)
1943

Reprinted by:

Janaway Publishing, Inc.
732 Kelsey Ct.
Santa Maria, CA 93454
(805) 925-1038
www.JanawayGenealogy.com

2014

ISBN: 978-1-59641-330-6

*Made in the United States of America*

BIBLIOGRAPHY

OF RESEARCH

PROJECTS REPORTS


CHECK LIST OF HISTORICAL RECORDS
SURVEY PUBLICATIONS


PREPARED BY

SARGENT B. CHILD

AND

DOROTHY P. HOLMES


ASSISTANCE IN CHECKING AND ARRANGING

BY

CYRIL E. PAQUIN


WPA TECHNICAL SERIES
RESEARCH AND RECORDS BIBLIOGRAPHY NO. 7

REVISED APRIL, 1943

FEDERAL WORKS AGENCY
WORK PROJECTS ADMINISTRATION
DIVISION OF SERVICE PROJECTS
WASHINGTON, D. C.

FOREWORD

This volume lists all publications of the several Historical Records Survey Projects programs of the Work Projects Administration, the issues of two related programs, the Survey of Federal Archives and the Inventory of American Imprints, and appendices in which is listed material pertinent to these programs. This is the final volume and supersedes WPA <u>Research and Records Bibliography No. 4</u>, issued September 12, 1940, and <u>Research and Records Bibliography No. 4, revised</u>, issued September 1, 1941.

As Historical Records Survey publications were issued in limited editions, their distribution was largely confined to a nationwide selection of libraries and certain regional depositories, which would make them available to a maximum number of users, each state project in addition sending copies to an intrastate list. The Library of Congress has assumed custodianship of surplus copies and although the supply is incomplete, depositories may be able to secure missing copies by addressing their requests to the Government Publications Reading Room, Library of Congress, Washington, D. C.

George H. Field
Deputy Commissioner of
Work Projects Administration

# PREFACE

This is a final listing of Historical Records Survey publications issued between 1936 and 1943. In a few States the Survey of Federal Archives and the American Imprints Inventory projects remained administratively separate from the Historical Records Survey, but followed the technical procedures established for the Survey. After September 1939, Survey publications in Arizona and Montana were issued under the names of the Arizona State Archival and Records Project and the Montana Inventory of Public Archives. In 1942, related Service Division projects in each State Work Projects Administration program were consolidated into one project known as the "War Services Project", in order to effect economies in operation as the number of available workers diminished. This explains the differing project names frequently appearing on the title pages of the publications listed.

Every attempt has been made to list all the Survey program publications issued in each State. It is anticipated, however, that in compiling this final listing of approximately 1,800 entries there is a small percentage of omissions.

Appendix I lists those records that were microfilmed as an incidental function of the respective State Historical Records Survey projects. This list does not include any other microfilming work done by the Work Projects Administration.

For those interested in the development of the Survey programs, Appendix II supplies a list of important articles and papers written by various members of the survey staff, and by others acquainted with the purpose, philosophy, techniques and results of the various phases of

v

the Survey program. Titles of technical manuals will be found in Appendix III, and published reports and summaries issued by a number of the State projects in Appendix IV.

A large amount of material gathered by the Survey was in varying stages of completion when the program was discontinued, a volume estimated to be eight or ten times greater than the volume of material represented by the publications listed in this final check list. State Work Projects Administration offices were instructed first to prepare detailed inventories and then to deposit the files of unpublished material in State depositories, where it would be most accessible for public use. Appendix V presents for most of the States the name and location of the depository in which these files are deposited. Copies of all available State lists of unpublished materials are located in the Library of Congress, The National Archives, and The Federal Works Agency Library, Washington, D. C.; in each State depository; and frequently are on deposit with State sponsors of the various State projects.

For the convenience of librarians who desire to obtain catalog cards for publications for which cards have been printed, the Library of Congress catalog card order numbers are supplied.

This listing supercedes all previous listings of <u>Historical Records Survey</u> publications.

# TABLE OF CONTENTS

|  | Pages |
|---|---|
| FOREWORD | iii |
| PREFACE | v |
| INVENTORIES OF FEDERAL ARCHIVES | 1 |
| FEDERAL ARCHIVES IN THE STATES – MISCELLANEOUS PUBLICATIONS | 13 |
| INVENTORIES OF STATE ARCHIVES | 15 |
| INVENTORIES OF COUNTY ARCHIVES | 17 |
| INVENTORIES OF MUNICIPAL AND TOWN ARCHIVES | 32 |
| TRANSCRIPTIONS OF PUBLIC ARCHIVES | 40 |
| VITAL STATISTICS | 43 |
| CHURCH ARCHIVES PUBLICATIONS – INVENTORIES | 49 |
| CHURCH ARCHIVES PUBLICATIONS – DIRECTORIES | 57 |
| MANUSCRIPTS PUBLICATIONS | 61 |
| AMERICAN IMPRINTS INVENTORIES | 70 |
| AMERICAN IMPRINTS INVENTORIES – NEWSPAPERS | 73 |
| AMERICAN PORTRAIT INVENTORIES | 75 |
| GUIDES TO CIVILIAN ORGANIZATIONS | 76 |
| MISCELLANEOUS PUBLICATIONS | 79 |
| MICROFILM (APPENDIX I) | 86 |
| PAPERS CONCERNING THE HISTORICAL RECORDS SURVEY APPENDIX (II) | 100 |
| MANUALS OF INSTRUCTIONS (APPENDIX III) | 104 |
| REPORTS, SUMMARIES AND MISCELLANEOUS (APPENDIX IV) | 106 |
| DEPOSITORIES OF UNPUBLISHED MATERIAL (APPENDIX V) | 108 |

INVENTORIES OF FEDERAL ARCHIVES IN THE STATES        39-29009

**ALABAMA:**
- II. The Federal Courts. (85 p., June 1940)
- III. The Department of The Treasury. (174 p., September 1940)
- IV. The Department of War. (150 p., December 1940)
- V. The Department of Justice. (45 p., June 1940)
- VI. The Post Office Department. Part 1. (210 p., September 1941)
- VII. The Department of the Navy. (10 p., April 1939)
- VIII. The Department of the Interior. (28 p., July 1941)
- IX. The Department of Agriculture. 3 Parts. (787 p., September 1941)
- X. The Department of Commerce. (32 p., December 1940)
- XII. The Veterans' Administration. (45 p., March 1941)
- XVI. The Farm Credit Administration. (17 p., June 1940)
- XVII. Miscellaneous Agencies. (264 p., March 1941)

**ARIZONA:**
- II. The Federal Courts. (29 p., September 1938)
- III. The Department of the Treasury. (41 p., March 1938)
- IV. The Department of War. (33 p., September 1938)
- V. The Department of Justice. (18 p., September 1938)
- VI. The Post Office Department. (36 p., March 1939)
- VII. The Department of the Navy. (2 p., September 1938)
- VIII. The Department of the Interior. (148 p., March 1939)
- IX. The Department of Agriculture. (202 p., January 1938)
- X. The Department of Commerce. (11 p., August 1938)
- XI. The Department of Labor. (66 p., September 1938)
- XII. The Veterans' Administration. (15 p., August 1938)
- XIII. The Civil Works Administration. (21 p., October 1938)
- XIV. The Emergency Relief Administration. (50 p., November 1938)
- XV. The Works Progress Administration. (72 p., November 1938)
- XVI. The Farm Credit Administration. (3 p., August 1938)
- XVII. Miscellaneous Agencies. (165 p., April 1939)

**ARKANSAS:**
- II. The Federal Courts. (53 p., January 1940)
- III. The Department of the Treasury. (25 p., June 1939)
- IV. The Department of War. (125 p., August 1938)
- V. The Department of Justice. (15 p., October 1938)
- VII. The Department of the Navy. (6 p., August 1938)
- VIII. The Department of the Interior. (8 p., August 1941)
- IX. The Department of Agriculture. (165 p., October 1939)
- X. The Department of Commerce. (8 p., October 1938)
- XI. The Department of Labor. (6 p., March 1940)
- XII. The Veterans' Administration. (46 p., October 1940)
- XV. The Works Progress Administration. (68 p., August 1941)
- XVI. The Farm Credit Administration. (8 p., August 1941)
- XVII. Miscellaneous Agencies. (29 p., August 1941)

---

*All inventories of Federal archives are mimeographed.

INVENTORIES OF FEDERAL ARCHIVES IN THE STATES (Cont'd)     39-29009

CALIFORNIA:
- II. The Federal Courts. (103 p., May 1939)
- III. The Department of the Treasury. 4 Parts. (844 p., November 1940)
- IV. The Department of War. Part 1. (296 p., February 1942)
- V. The Department of Justice. (108 p., May 1940)
- VIII. The Department of the Interior. 2 Parts. (437 p., May 1941)
- IX. The Department of Agriculture. 3 Parts. (728 p., June 1940)
- X. The Department of Commerce. (139 p., May 1939)
- XI. The Department of Labor. (331 p, June 1940)

COLORADO:
- II. The Federal Courts. (36 p., October 1939)
- III. The Department of the Treasury. (149 p., May 1939)
- IV. The Department of War. (90 p., May 1938)
- V. The Department of Justice. (22 p., October 1939)
- VII. The Department of the Navy. (9 p., December 1938)
- IX. The Department of Agriculture. 3 Parts. (538 p., August 1940)
- X. The Department of Commerce. (10 p., December 1941)
- XI. The Department of Labor. (33 p., September 1940)

CONNECTICUT:
- II. The Federal Courts. (29 p., June 1939)
- III. The Department of the Treasury. 2 Parts. (544 p., March 1941)
- IV. The Department of War. (63 p., May 1939)
- V. The Department of Justice. (17 p., March 1940)
- VII. The Department of the Navy. (76 p., May 1939)
- VIII. The Department of the Interior. (13 p., December 1939)
- IX. The Department of Agriculture. (199 p., June 1940)
- X. The Department of Commerce. (27 p., June 1940)
- XI. The Department of Labor. (25 p., December 1940)
- XII. The Veterans' Administration. (42 p., June 1940)
- XIII. The Civil Works Administration. (12 p., December 1939)
- XVII. Miscellaneous Agencies. (84 p., March 1940)

DELAWARE:
- II. The Federal Courts. (6 p., December 1941)
- V. The Department of Justice. (3 p., March 1942)
- IX. The Department of Agriculture. (47 p., December 1941)
- X. The Department of Commerce. (32 p., February 1942)
- XI. The Department of Labor. (10 p., April 1942)
- XVI. The Farm Credit Administration. (10 p., March 1941)

FLORIDA:
- II. The Federal Courts. (67 p., May 1940)
- III. The Department of the Treasury. (240 p., May 1941)
- IV. The Department of War. (176 p., May 1940)
- V. The Department of Justice. (43 p., April 1941)
- VII. The Department of the Navy. (177 p., March 1941)
- VIII. The Department of the Interior. (28 p., October 1941)

INVENTORIES OF FEDERAL ARCHIVES IN THE STATES (Cont'd)   39-29009

FLORIDA: (Cont'd)
    IX. The Department of Agriculture. (203 p., May 1941)
    X. The Department of Commerce. (40 p., April 1941)
    XI. The Department of Labor. (56 p., April 1941)
    XII. The Veterans' Administration. (28 p., February 1941)
    XVI. The Farm Credit Administration. (34 p., March 1941)
    XVII. Miscellaneous Agencies. (58 p., July 1941)

GEORGIA:
    II. The Federal Courts. (105 p., December 1940)
    III. The Department of the Treasury. (161 p., June 1939)
    IV. The Department of War. (396 p., January 1941)
    V. The Department of Justice. (130 p., August 1939)
    VII. The Department of the Navy. (21 p., May 1939)
    VIII. The Department of the Interior. (14 p., November 1941)
    IX. The Department of Agriculture. Part 2. (253 p., June 1941) Part 4. (77 p., April 1941)
    XVI. The Farm Credit Administration. (33 p., February 1941)
    XVII. Miscellaneous Agencies. (197 p., October 1941)

IDAHO:
    V. The Department of Justice. (18 p., June 1939)
    IX. The Department of Agriculture. (316 p., September 1939)
    X. The Department of Commerce. (22 p., June 1939)

ILLINOIS:
    II. The Federal Courts. (139 p., March 1940)
    III. The Department of the Treasury. (283 p., March 1940)
    IV. The Department of War. 2 Parts. (747 p., January 1941)
    V. The Department of Justice. (60 p., June 1940)
    VII. The Department of the Navy. (177 p., March 1940)
    VIII. The Department of the Interior. (110 p., March 1941)
    IX. The Department of Agriculture. 2 Parts. (344 p., January 1939)
    X. The Department of Commerce. (26 p., January 1939)
    XI. The Department of Labor. (69 p., May 1941)
    XII. The Veterans' Administration. (133 p., August 1941)
    XVI. The Farm Credit Administration. (12 p., May 1941)
    XVII. Miscellaneous Agencies. (172 p., August 1941)

INDIANA:
    II. The Federal Courts. (44 p., March 1939)
    III. The Department of the Treasury. (65 p., November 1938)
    IV. The Department of War. (143 p., January 1939)
    V. The Department of Justice. (20 p., October 1938)
    VII. The Department of the Navy. (9 p., February 1939)
    VIII. The Department of the Interior. (24 p., April 1939)
    IX. The Department of Agriculture. (393 p., March 1939)
    X. The Department of Commerce. (20 p., October 1938)
    XI. The Department of Labor. (47 p., March 1939)
    XII. The Veterans' Administration. (51 p., February 1939)
    XIII. The Civil Works Administration. (97 p., July 1939)
    XIV. The Emergency Relief Administration. (115 p., October 1939)

## INVENTORIES OF FEDERAL ARCHIVES IN THE STATES (Cont'd)

**INDIANA:** (Cont'd)
- XV. The Works Progress Administration. 2 Parts. (425 p., April 1941)
- XVI. The Farm Credit Administration. (21 p., April 1939)
- XVII. Miscellaneous Agencies. 2 Parts. (417 p., October 1940)

**IOWA:**
- II. The Federal Courts. (69 p., May 1940)
- III. The Department of the Treasury. (74 p., February 1939)
- IV. The Department of War. (92 p., July 1940)
- V. The Department of Justice. (15 p., June 1939)
- VII. The Department of the Navy. (13 p., June 1939)
- VIII. The Department of the Interior. (22 p., October 1940)
- IX. The Department of Agriculture. (327 p., May 1940)
- X. The Department of Commerce. (32 p., November 1938)
- XVI. The Farm Credit Administration. (39 p., January 1940)

**KANSAS:**
- II. The Federal Courts. (22 p., February 1939)
- III. The Department of the Treasury. (46 p., December 1938)
- IV. The Department of War. (45 p., February 1939)
- V. The Department of Justice. (15 p., May 1939)
- VII. The Department of the Navy. (8 p., May 1939)
- VIII. The Department of the Interior. (22 p., February 1940)
- IX. The Department of Agriculture. (182 p., February 1940)
- X. The Department of Commerce. (11 p., August 1940)
- XI. The Department of Labor. (39 p., April 1941)
- XII. The Veterans' Administration. (31 p., June 1941)
- XVI. The Farm Credit Administration. (45 p., May 1940)
- XVII. Miscellaneous Agencies. (51 p., March 1941)

**KENTUCKY:**
- II. The Federal Courts. (89 p., November 1939)
- III. The Department of the Treasury. (131 p., June 1939)
- IV. The Department of War. (132 p., March 1941)
- V. The Department of Justice. (16 p., September 1938)
- VII. The Department of the Navy. (9 p., January 1939)
- IX. The Department of Agriculture. (125 p., October 1940)
- XI. The Department of Labor. (23 p., May 1939)
- XVI. The Farm Credit Administration. (20 p., November 1938)

**LOUISIANA:**
- II. The Federal Courts. (56 p., November 1939)
- III. The Department of the Treasury. (361 p., December 1938)
- IV. The Department of War. (232 p., September 1939)
- V. The Department of Justice. (23 p., October 1938)
- VII. The Department of the Navy. (49 p., July 1938)
- VIII. The Department of the Interior. (53 p., August 1941)
- IX. The Department of Agriculture. (308 p., July 1938)
- X. The Department of Commerce. (92 p., June 1939)
- XI. The Department of Labor. (23 p., June 1940)
- XII. The Veterans' Administration. (44 p., June 1940)
- XIII. The Civil Works Administration. (15 p., November 1941)

INVENTORIES OF FEDERAL ARCHIVES IN THE STATES (Cont'd)          39-29009

LOUISIANA: (Cont'd)
    XIV. Emergency Relief Administration. (23 p., June 1941)
    XV. The Works Progress Administration. (42 p., June 1941)
    XVI. The Farm Credit Administration. (14 p., April 1939)
    XVII. Miscellaneous Agencies. (128 p., June 1941)

MARYLAND:
    II. The Federal Courts. (45 p., February 1939)
    III. The Department of the Treasury. (272 p., February 1939)
    IV. The Department of War. (336 p., June 1939)
    V. The Department of Justice. (16 p., August 1938)
    VII. The Department of the Navy. (70 p., December 1938)
    VIII. The Department of the Interior. (19 p., February 1939)
    IX. The Department of Agriculture. (177 p., October 1938)
    X. The Department of Commerce. (62 p., December 1938)
    XI. The Department of Labor. (25 p., August 1938)
    XII. The Veterans' Administration. (79 p., August 1939)
    XVI. The Farm Credit Administration. (27 p., August 1939)
    XVII. Miscellaneous Agencies. 2 Parts. (335 p., March 1940)

MASSACHUSETTS:
    II. The Federal Courts. (44 p., July 1938)
    III. The Department of the Treasury. 3 Parts. (734 p., January 1939)
    IV. The Department of War. (466 p., May 1939)
    V. The Department of Justice. (26 p., September 1938)
    VII. The Department of the Navy. (171 p., July 1938)
    VIII. The Department of the Interior. (14 p., July 1938)
    IX. The Department of Agriculture. (115 p., July 1938)
    X. The Department of Commerce. (83 p., August 1938)
    XI. The Department of Labor. (84 p., June 1939)
    XII. The Veterans' Administration. (46 p., December 1940)
    XIV. The Emergency Relief Administration. (141 p., April 1941)
    XVI. The Farm Credit Administration. (15 p., May 1939)
    XVII. Miscellaneous Agencies. (128 p., August 1940)

MICHIGAN:
    II. The Federal Courts. (51 p., June 1938)
    III. The Department of the Treasury. (298 p., July 1939)
    IV. The Department of War. 2 Parts. (286 p., December 1939)
    V. The Department of Justice. (41 p., June 1938)
    VII. The Department of the Navy. (34 p., December 1939)
    VIII. The Department of the Interior. (18 p., January 1941)
    IX. The Department of Agriculture. (205 p., December 1939)
    X. The Department of Commerce. (87 p., December 1939)
    XI. The Department of Labor. (100 p., December 1939)
    XII. The Veterans' Administration. (50 p., August 1940)
    XVI. The Farm Credit Administration. (38 p., June 1940)
    XVII. Miscellaneous Agencies. (346 p., February 1942)

## INVENTORIES OF FEDERAL ARCHIVES IN THE STATES (Cont'd)

**MINNESOTA:**
- II. The Federal Courts. (55 p., June 1939)
- III. The Department of the Treasury. (175 p., December 1938)
- IV. The Department of War. (133 p., March 1940)
- V. The Department of Justice. (32 p., March 1940)
- VII. The Department of the Navy. (21 p., December 1938)
- VIII. The Department of the Interior. (190 p., November 1941)
- IX. The Department of Agriculture. 2 Parts. (366 p., September 1938)
- X. The Department of Commerce. (24 p., May 1939)
- XI. The Department of Labor. (101 p., August 1940)
- XII. The Veterans' Administration. (55 p., May 1940)
- XVI. The Farm Credit Administration. (67 p., April 1939)
- XVII. Miscellaneous Agencies. (221 p., January 1941)

**MISSISSIPPI:**
- II. The Federal Courts. (59 p., January 1940)
- III. The Department of the Treasury. (49 p., March 1940)
- IV. The Department of War. (99 p., October 1938)
- V. The Department of Justice. (17 p., October 1939)
- VII. The Department of the Navy. (4 p., August 1938)
- VIII. The Department of the Interior. (21 p., August 1941)
- IX. The Department of Agriculture. (240 p., December 1939)
- X. The Department of Commerce. (10 p., October 1938)
- XI. The Department of Labor. (32 p., June 1940)
- XII. The Veterans' Administration. (35 p., June 1940)
- XIII. The Civil Works Administration. (7 p., June 1941)
- XIV The Emergency Relief Administration. (17 p., June 1941)
- XV. The Works Progress Administration. (81 p., August 1941)
- XVI. The Farm Credit Administration. (9 p., June 1940)
- XVII. Miscellaneous Agencies. (32 p., June 1941)

**MISSOURI:**
- II. The Federal Courts. (65 p., December 1938)
- III. The Department of the Treasury. (164 p., December 1938)
- IV. The Department of War. (125 p., December 1938)
- V. The Department of Justice. (46 p., December 1937)
- VII. The Department of the Navy. (17 p., December 1938)
- VIII. The Department of the Interior. (31 p., December 1938)
- IX. The Department of Agriculture. (230 p., December 1938)
- X. The Department of Commerce. (23 p., December 1938)
- XI. The Department of Labor. (69 p., December 1938)
- XII. The Veterans' Administration. (38 p., December 1938)
- XIII. The Civil Works Administration. (18 p., December 1938)
- XIV. The Emergency Relief Administration. (58 p., December 1938)
- XV. The Works Progress Administration. (137 p., December 1938)
- XVI. The Farm Credit Administration. (19 p., December 1938)
- XVII. Miscellaneous Agencies. (177 p., December 1938)

INVENTORIES OF FEDERAL ARCHIVES IN THE STATES (Cont'd)   39-29009

MONTANA:
    II.    The Federal Courts. (31 p., January 1941)
    IV.    The Department of War. (72 p., January 1941)
    IX.    The Department of Agriculture. (155 p., July 1939)
    X.    The Department of Commerce. (9 p., July 1939)
    XII.    The Veterans' Administration. (24 p., November 1940)
    XVI.    The Farm Credit Administration. (11 p., July 1939)

NEBRASKA:
    II.    The Federal Courts. (29 p., June 1939)
    III.    The Department of the Treasury. (56 p., April 1939)
    IV.    The Department of War. (96 p., May 1940)
    V.    The Department of Justice. (13 p., June 1939)
    VII.    The Department of the Navy. (7 p., May 1939)
    VIII.    The Department of the Interior. (20 p., June 1939)
    IX.    The Department of Agriculture. (165 p., March 1940)
    X.    The Department of Commerce. (16 p., November 1938)
    XI.    The Department of Labor. (23 p., September 1941)
    XII.    The Veterans' Administration. (10 p., June 1939)
    XVI.    The Farm Credit Administration. (54 p., February 1940)
    XVII.    Miscellaneous Agencies. (69 p., April 1941)

NEVADA:
    II.    The Federal Courts. (25 p., April 1940)
    III.    The Department of the Treasury. (22 p., March 1940)
    IV.    The Department of War. (10 p., May 1941)
    V.    The Department of Justice. (15 p., May 1940)
    VII.    The Department of the Navy. (21 p., March 1940)
    VIII.    The Department of the Interior. (178 p., July 1940)
    IX.    The Department of Agriculture. (125 p., February 1941)
    XI.    The Department of Labor. (32 p., May 1941)
    XII.    The Veterans' Administration. (14 p., October 1941)
    XVI.    The Farm Credit Administration. (5 p., August 1941)
    XVII.    Miscellaneous Agencies. (22 p., October 1941)

NEW HAMPSHIRE:
    II.    The Federal Courts. (8 p., June 1941)
    III.    The Department of the Treasury. (41 p., July 1938)
    IV.    The Department of War. (42 p., October 1938)
    V.    The Department of Justice. (8 p., September 1938)
    VII.    The Department of the Navy. (5 p., September 1939)
    VIII.    The Department of the Interior. (4 p., June 1941)
    IX.    The Department of Agriculture. (71 p., June 1938)
    X.    The Department of Commerce. (11 p., September 1938)
    XI.    The Department of Labor. (19 p., February 1941)
    XII.    The Veterans' Administration. (10 p., October 1938)
    XV.    The Works Progress Administration. (32 p., April 1939)
    XVI.    The Farm Credit Administration. (5 p., December 1938)
    XVII.    Miscellaneous Agencies. (133 p., June 1941)

INVENTORIES OF FEDERAL ARCHIVES IN THE STATES (Cont'd)    39-29009

NEW JERSEY:
- III. The Department of the Treasury. (271 p., November 1939)
- IV. The Department of War. (209 p., September 1940)
- V. The Department of Justice. (20 p., December 1941)
- VII. The Department of the Navy. (154 p., April 1940)
- VIII. The Department of the Interior. (23 p., October 1940)
- IX. The Department of Agriculture. (221 p., July 1939)
- X. The Department of Commerce. (51 p., October 1940)
- XI. The Department of Labor. (67 p., October 1940)
- XII. The Veterans' Administration. (38 p., September 1940)
- XVI. The Farm Credit Administration. (10 p., February 1941)
- XVII. Miscellaneous Agencies. (190 p., January 1941)

NEW MEXICO:
- II. The Federal Courts. (14 p., April 1941)
- III. The Department of the Treasury. (40 p., February 1941)
- IV. The Department of War. (13 p., January 1941)
- V. The Department of Justice. (23 p., December 1940)
- VII. The Department of the Navy. (7 p., December 1940)
- XII. The Veterans' Administration. (40 p., December 1940)
- XIII. The Civil Works Administration. (10 p., January 1941)

NEW YORK:
- II. The Federal Courts. (174 p., November 1939)
- III. The Department of the Treasury. 3 Parts. (1482 p., June 1940)
- IV. The Department of War. 2 Parts. (1233 p., November 1941)
- V. The Department of Justice. (119 p., November 1939)
- VII. The Department of the Navy. (546 p., September 1940)
- VIII. The Department of the Interior. (46 p., January 1942)
- IX. The Department of Agriculture. (446 p., June 1939)
- X. The Department of Commerce. (156 p., April 1941)
- XI. The Department of Labor. (186 p., December 1941)
- XII. The Veterans' Administration. (157 p., September 1941)
- XVII. Miscellaneous Agencies. (117 p., December 1941)

NORTH CAROLINA:
- II. The Federal Courts. (102 p., April 1940)
- III. The Department of the Treasury. (151 p., June 1939)
- IV. The Department of War. (91 p., June 1940)
- V. The Department of Justice. (32 p., October 1939)
- VII. The Department of the Navy. (12 p., June 1939)
- VIII. The Department of the Interior. (36 p., July 1940)
- IX. The Department of Agriculture. 3 Parts. (423 p., June 1939)
- X. The Department of Commerce. (32 p., December 1939)
- XI. The Department of Labor. (10 p., August 1940)
- XII. The Veterans' Administration. (18 p., July 1940)
- XIII. The Civil Works Administration. (16 p., March 1941)
- XV. The Works Progress Administration. (158 p., March 1941)
- XVI. The Farm Credit Administration. (26 p., August 1940)
- XVII. Miscellaneous Agencies. (130 p., October 1940)

INVENTORIES OF FEDERAL ARCHIVES IN THE STATES (Cont'd)         39-29009

NORTH DAKOTA:
- II. The Federal Courts. (23 p., April 1941)
- III. The Department of the Treasury. (62 p., February 1941)
- IV. The Department of War. (17 p., March 1941)
- V. The Department of Justice. (7 p., April 1941)
- VII. The Department of the Navy. (5 p., May 1941)
- VIII. The Department of the Interior. (104 p., March 1942)
- IX. The Department of Agriculture. (343 p., February 1942)
- XVII. Miscellaneous Agencies. Part 1. (50 p., February 1942)

OHIO:
- II. The Federal Courts. (96 p., September 1940)
- III. The Department of the Treasury. 2 Parts. (416 p., December 1940)
- V. The Department of Justice. (55 p., June 1940)
- VII. The Department of the Navy. (32 p., February 1939)
- VIII. The Department of the Interior. (7 p., August 1941)
- X. The Department of Commerce. (30 p., March 1939)
- XVI. The Farm Credit Administration. (14 p., April 1939)

OKLAHOMA:
- II. The Federal Courts. (60 p., June 1939)
- III. The Department of the Treasury. (60 p., June 1938)
- IV. The Department of War. (158 p., June 1939)
- V. The Department of Justice. (97 p., May 1939)
- VII. The Department of the Navy. (11 p., May 1939)
- IX. The Department of Agriculture. (313 p., November 1938)
- X. The Department of Commerce. (6 p., May 1940)
- XI. The Department of Labor. (35 p., November 1938)
- XII. The Veterans' Administration. (34 p., May 1940)
- XIV. The Emergency Relief Administration. (36 p., December 1940)
- XV. The Works Progress Administration. (89 p., November 1939)
- XVI. The Farm Credit Administration. (41 p., September 1938)
- XVII. Miscellaneous Agencies. (110 p., October 1940)

OREGON:
- II. The Federal Courts. (37 p., June 1939)
- III. The Department of the Treasury. (330 p., March 1941)
- IV. The Department of War. (163 p., May 1940)
- V. The Department of Justice. (28 p., June 1939)
- VII. The Department of the Navy. (29 p., April 1940)
- VIII. The Department of the Interior. (441 p., October 1941)
- X. The Department of Commerce. (90 p., September 1941)
- XI. The Department of Labor. (108 p., February 1939)
- XII. The Veterans' Administration. (70 p., March 1940)
- XIII. The Civil Works Administration. (15 p., April 1941)
- XIV. The Emergency Relief Administration. (26 p., 1941)
- XV. The Works Progress Administration. (102 p., March 1941)
- XVI. The Farm Credit Administration. (10 p., April 1940)
- XVII. Miscellaneous Agencies. (258 p., January 1941)

## INVENTORIES OF FEDERAL ARCHIVES IN THE STATES (Cont'd)

39-29009

PENNSYLVANIA:
- II. The Federal Courts. (71 p., March 1940)
- III. The Department of the Treasury. 2 Parts. (401 p., June 1941)
- IV. The Department of War. 2 Parts. (481 p., April 1941)
- V. The Department of Justice. (38 p., March 1940)
- VII. The Department of the Navy. (243 p., June 1940)
- VIII. The Department of the Interior. (49 p., April 1941)
- IX. The Department of Agriculture. 2 Parts. (341 p., June 1941)
- X. The Department of Commerce. (37 p., May 1940)
- XI. The Department of Labor. (173 p., 1942)
- XII. The Veterans' Administration. (43 p., March 1941)
- XVI. The Farm Credit Administration. (12 p., April 1941)

RHODE ISLAND:
- II. The Federal Courts. (40 p., May 1938)
- III. The Department of the Treasury. (377 p., December 1938)
- IV. The Department of War. (277 p., December 1938)
- V. The Department of Justice. (13 p., August 1938)
- VII. The Department of the Navy. (335 p., March 1939)
- VIII. The Department of the Interior. (11 p., May 1938)
- IX. The Department of Agriculture. (125 p., February 1939)
- X. The Department of Commerce. (59 p., April 1938)
- XI. The Department of Labor. (54 p., November 1938)
- XII. The Veterans' Administration. (31 p., January 1939)
- XVI. The Farm Credit Administration. (5 p., April 1938)
- XVII. Miscellaneous Agencies. 2 Parts. (14 p., May 1938)

SOUTH CAROLINA:
- III. The Department of the Treasury. (111 p., July 1939)
- IV. The Department of War. (31 p., February 1942)
- V. The Department of Justice. (18 p., June 1939)

SOUTH DAKOTA:
- II. The Federal Courts. (18 p., October 1941)
- III. The Department of the Treasury. (15 p., December 1941)
- IV. The Department of War. (19 p., October 1941)
- VII. The Department of the Navy. (4 p., October 1941)
- VIII. The Department of the Interior. (157 p., March 1942)
- XVII. Miscellaneous Agencies. (39 p., February 1942)

TENNESSEE:
- II. The Federal Courts. (96 p., April 1940)
- III. The Department of the Treasury. (98 p., July 1939)
- IV. The Department of War. (91 p., July 1939)
- V. The Department of Justice. (37 p., November 1939)
- VII. The Department of the Navy. (9 p., July 1938)
- VIII. The Department of the Interior. (53 p., February 1941)
- IX. The Department of Agriculture. (187 p., September 1938)
- X. The Department of Commerce. (10 p., June 1940)

INVENTORIES OF FEDERAL ARCHIVES IN THE STATES (Cont'd)   39-29009

TENNESSEE: (Cont'd)
    XI. The Department of Labor. (25 p., August 1941)
    XII. The Veterans' Administration. (39 p., June 1941)
    XIV. The Emergency Relief Administration. (51 p., June 1941)
    XV. The Works Progress Administration. (207 p., June 1941)
    XVI. The Farm Credit Administration. (51 p., April 1941)
    XVII. Miscellaneous Agencies. (85 p., May 1941)

TEXAS:
    II. The Federal Courts. 4 Parts. (275 p., June 1939)
    III. The Department of the Treasury. 4 Parts. (384 p., June 1939)
    IV. The Department of War. 12 Parts. (1364 p., June 1939)
    V. The Department of Justice. (70 p., June 1939)
    VII. The Department of the Navy. (24 p., June 1939)
    VIII. The Department of the Interior. (114 p., January 1941)
    IX. The Department of Agriculture. 9 Parts. (1815 p., June 1940)
    X. The Department of Commerce. (75 p., June 1939)
    XI. The Department of Labor. 2 Parts. (539 p., October 1940)
    XII. The Veterans' Administration. (97 p., December 1940)
    XVI. The Farm Credit Administration. (81 p., June 1940)
    XVII. Miscellaneous Agencies. 2 Parts. (482 p., October 1940)

UTAH:
    II. The Federal Courts. (17 p., October 1939)
    III. The Department of the Treasury. (80 p., October 1939)
    IV. The Department of War. (46 p., June 1940)
    V. The Department of Justice. (20 p., October 1939)
    VII. The Department of the Navy. (9 p., February 1940)
    VIII. The Department of the Interior. (146 p., September 1940)
    IX. The Department of Agriculture. (274 p., February 1940)
    X. The Department of Commerce. (34 p., May 1940)
    XI. The Department of Labor. (46 p., September 1940)
    XII. The Veterans' Administration. (30 p., April 1940)
    XVI. The Farm Credit Administration. (24 p., May 1940)

VERMONT:
    II. The Federal Courts. (17 p., December 1939)
    III. The Department of the Treasury. (129 p., September 1939)
    IV. The Department of War. (114 p., December 1938)
    V. The Department of Justice. (14 p., December 1938)
    VII. The Department of the Navy. (4 p., March 1939)
    IX. The Department of Agriculture. (141 p., October 1939)
    X. The Department of Commerce. (25 p., April 1940)
    XI. The Department of Labor. (90 p., February 1941)
    XII. The Veterans' Administration. (11 p., December 1939)
    XVII. Miscellaneous Agencies. 3 Parts. (350 p., August 1941)

VIRGINIA:
    II. The Federal Courts. (167 p., May 1942)
    V. The Department of Justice. (37 p., January 1941)
    IX. The Department of Agriculture. (436 p., June 1941)

## INVENTORIES OF FEDERAL ARCHIVES IN THE STATES (Cont'd)

**WASHINGTON:**
- II. The Federal Courts. (91 p., March 1940)
- IV. The Department of War. (777 p., November 1941)
- V. The Department of Justice. (47 p., March 1940)
- VII. The Department of the Navy. (493 p., March 1941)
- VIII. The Department of the Interior. (364 p., February 1942)
- X. The Department of Commerce. (224 p., December 1941)
- XI. The Department of Labor. (184 p., December 1941)
- XII. The Veterans' Administration. (105 p., August 1941)
- XIII. The Civil Works Administration. (21 p., April 1941)
- XV. The Works Progress Administration. (265 p., December 1941)
- XVI. The Farm Credit Administration. (38 p., May 1940)

**WEST VIRGINIA:**
- III. The Department of the Treasury. (65 p., December 1938)
- IV. The Department of War. (77 p., March 1939)
- VII. The Department of the Navy. (12 p., July 1939)
- IX. The Department of Agriculture. (149 p., February 1939)

**WISCONSIN:**
- II. The Federal Courts. (37 p., October 1939)
- III. The Department of the Treasury. (186 p., May 1939)
- IV. The Department of War. (66 p., January 1939)
- V. The Department of Justice. (24 p., March 1939)
- VII. The Department of the Navy. (14 p., January 1939)
- VIII. The Department of the Interior. (110 p., October 1939)
- IX. The Department of Agriculture. (328 p., May 1939)
- X. The Department of Commerce. (57 p., March 1939)
- XII. The Veterans' Administration. (51 p., January 1939)
- XIII. The Civil Works Administration. (23 p., October 1939)
- XV. The Works Progress Administration. (149 p., July 1939)
- XVII. Miscellaneous Agencies. (67 p., February 1941)

**WYOMING:**
- III. The Department of the Treasury. (21 p., February 1939)
- IV. The Department of War. (153 p., June 1939)
- V. The Department of Justice. (10 p., January 1939)
- VII. The Department of the Navy. (6 p., January 1939)
- IX. The Department of Agriculture. (151 p., June 1939)
- XI. The Department of Labor. (30 p., October 1940)

## FEDERAL ARCHIVES IN THE STATES: MISCELLANEOUS PUBLICATIONS

CALIFORNIA:
    Ship Registers and Enrollments of Eureka, California.
        (166 p., August 1941)

LOUISIANA:
    A History of the U. S. Custom House at New Orleans, Louisiana.   41-52363
        (60 p., April 1940)

    Ship Registers and Enrollments of New Orleans:                42-14127
        Vol. I,   1804-1820.  (186 p., August 1941)
        Vol. II,  1821-1830.  (209 p., February 1942)
        Vol.III,  1831-1840.  (291 p., March 1942)
        Vol. IV,  1841-1850.  (378 p., March 1942)
        Vol. V,   1851-1860.  (351 p., March 1942)
        Vol. VI,  1861-1870.  (363 p., March 1942)

MAINE:
    Ship Registers and Enrollments of Machias, Maine, 1780-1930.   42-50709
        Part 1. (593 p., March 1942)

    Ship Registers and Enrollments of Saco, Maine, 1791-1915.    42-50710
        (122 p., 1942)

MASSACHUSETTS:
    The Eleven Original Customs Districts Established in the Commonwealth of Massachusetts. (16 p., 1941)

    Ship Registers and Enrollments of Boston and Charlestown:     42-21043
        Vol. I, 1789-1795. (248 p., March 1942)

    Ship Registers of the District of Barnstable, Massachusetts,
        1814-1913. (173 p., 1938)

    Ship Registers of the District of Plymouth, Massachusetts,     40-26535
        1789-1808. (218 p., May 1939)

    Ship Registers of the District of Dighton-Fall River,
        Massachusetts, 1789-1938. (190 p., July 1939)

    Ship Registers of New Bedford:                                 40-29051
        Vol. I,   1796-1815. (427 p., July 1939)
        Vol. II,  1815-1865. (357 p., January 1941)
        Vol.III,  1866-1939. (256 p., January 1941)

NEW JERSEY:
    Description of Post Office Department Forms. (45 p., June 1940)

## FEDERAL ARCHIVES IN THE STATES: MISCELLANEOUS PUBLICATIONS (Cont'd)

**OREGON:**

    Guide to Federal Agencies Maintained and Operating in the State 42-51760
        of Oregon. (177 p., May 1942)

    Ship Registers and Enrollments of Marshfield, Oregon, 1873-1941.
        (86 p., April 1942)

    Ship Registers and Enrollments of Portland, Oregon, 1867-1941.
        (288 p., June 1942)

**PENNSYLVANIA:**

    Ship Registers of Port of Philadelphia:
        Vol. I, A-D. (293 p., 1942)

**RHODE ISLAND:**

    Ship Registers and Enrollments of Providence, Rhode Island,    42-1204
        1773-1939.
        Vol. I, A-M. (p. 1-766, 1941)
        Vol. I, N-Z. (p. 775-1516, 1941)

    Ship Registers and Enrollments of Bristol-Warren, Rhode Island,
        1773-1939. (435 p., 1941)

    Ship Registers and Enrollments of Newport, Rhode Island,    42-1203
        1790-1939:
        Vol. I. (810 p., 1941)
        Vol. II. (389 p., 1941)

**WISCONSIN:**

    A Directory to United States Government Agencies in Wisconsin.
    (107 p., April 1938)

## INVENTORIES OF STATE ARCHIVES

CALIFORNIA, NORTHERN:
    Department of Industrial Relations:                                            41-52830
        Division of Immigration and Housing. (vi, 47 p. mimeo.,
        April 1941)

ILLINOIS:
    Series III. State Council of Defense of Illinois, 1917-1919.   42-14201
        (ix, 53 p. mimeo., January 1942)

LOUISIANA:
    Series II. The Judiciary:                                                             41-52965
        No. 1. The Superior Court of the Territory of Orleans.
            (ix, 37 p. mimeo., February 1942)

        No. 2. The Supreme Court of Louisiana. (vii, 59 p.
            mimeo., April 1941)
        No. 3. The Courts of Appeal of Louisiana. (v, 97 p.
            mimeo., September 1941)

    Series III. The Executive:
        No. 2. The Lieutenant Governor. (v, 11 p. mimeo.,
            November 1941)

MICHIGAN:
    State Police. (v, 46 p. mimeo., August 1941)                   42-1465

NORTH CAROLINA:
    Series I. General Governmental Agencies:                          40-31688
        No. 7. State Planning Board. (vi, 7 p. mimeo.,
            March 1942)
    Series II. Agencies of Fiscal Control:
        No. 4. Local Government Commission. (iv, 32 p. mimeo.,
            March 1941)

    Series IV. Regulatory Agencies:
        No. 1. Utilities Commission. (vi, 72 p. mimeo.,
            March 1942)
        No. 3. Insurance Department. (iv, 78 p. mimeo.,
            August 1940)
        No. 4. State Board of Alcoholic Control. (iv, 12 p.
            mimeo., November, 1939)
        No. 5-27. Licensing Boards. (vii, 123 p. mimeo.,
            June 1941)

    Series VIII. Social Service Agencies:
        No. 1. North Carolina Board of Health. (vi, 121 p.
            mimeo., December 1941)
        No. 20. Stonewall Jackson Manual Training and Industrial
            School. (iv, 12 p. mimeo., January 1941)

## INVENTORIES OF STATE ARCHIVES (Cont'd)

**NORTH CAROLINA:** (Cont'd)
    SERIES IX. Miscellaneous Agencies:
        No. 1. North Carolina Historical Commission. (iv, 13 p. mimeo., September 1940)
        Nos. 2-4. State Library, Library Commission of North Carolina, and State Board of Elections. (vii, 27 p. mimeo., November 1941)
        No. 3. Library Commission of North Carolina. (see Nos. 2-4)
        No. 4. State Board of Elections. (see Nos. 2-4)
        No. 5. Board of Advisors of the Veteran Loan Fund. (iv, 22 p. mimeo., August 1940)
        No. 10. North Carolina Rural Electrification Authority. (iv, 9 p. mimeo., January 1940)

**OHIO:**
    Secretary of State. (v, 71 p. mimeo., July 1940)     40-28597

**OKLAHOMA:**
    A List of Records of the State of Oklahoma. (iv, 272 p. mimeo., December 1938)     39-26139

**UTAH:**
    The State of Deseret. (187 p. printed 1940) (Reprinted A-41-2152 Rev. from Utah State Historical Society, State Capitol, Salt Lake City, Vol. 8 (2-3-4), April, July, October, 1940, pp. 65-251)

**WISCONSIN:**
    Department of State. (vii, 265 p. mimeo., January 1942)     42-16941 Rev.
    Banking Department. (vii, 325 p. mimeo., 1942)     42-20200 Rev.
    Treasury Department. (vi, 232 p. mimeo., 1942)

## INVENTORIES OF COUNTY ARCHIVES

**ALABAMA:** 40-33755
- No. 14. Clay. (xii, 179 p. mimeo., December 1941)
- No. 17. Colbert. (v, 333 p. mimeo., May 1939)
- No. 18. Conecuh. (iv, 127 p. mimeo., May 1938)
- No. 22. Cullman. (xvii, 201 p. mimeo., December 1941)
- No. 32. Greene. Prelim. edition. (xii, 134 p. mimeo., February 1942)
- No. 33. Hale. (vi, 147 p. mimeo., July 1940)
- No. 39. Lauderdale. Prelim. edition. (xi, 127 p. mimeo., June 1942)
- No. 43. Lowndes. (vi, 401 p. mimeo., November 1939)
- No. 45. Madison. Prelim. edition. (xiv, 379 p. mimeo., June 1942)
- No. 46. Marengo. (xii, 205 p. mimeo., August 1940)
- No. 60. Sumter. (xi, 204 p. mimeo., August 1940)
- No. 61. Talladega. (iii, 435 p. mimeo., April 1940)
- No. 66. Wilcox. Prelim. edition. (xii, 122 p. mimeo., February 1942)
- No. 67. Winston. Prelim. edition. (xii, 108 p. mimeo., December 1941)

**ARIZONA:**
- No. 7. Maricopa. (vi, 438 p. mimeo., August 1940)
- No. 10. Pima. (vi, 207 p. mimeo., July 1938)
- No. 12. Santa Cruz. (x, 313 p. mimeo., November 1941)

**ARKANSAS:** 40-31685
- No. 3. Baxter. (xi, 73 p. mimeo., February 1942)
- No. 4. Benton. (xiii, 112 p. mimeo., December 1941)
- No. 8. Carroll. (xviii, 118 p. mimeo., May 1942)
- No. 12. Cleburne. (v, 217 p. mimeo., March 1939)
- No. 13. Cleveland. (xi, 113 p. mimeo., April 1941)
- No. 19. Cross. (xi, 114 p. mimeo., July 1940)
- No. 23. Faulkner. (v, 251 p. mimeo., December 1939)
- No. 30. Hot Springs. (v, 121 p. mimeo., March 1940)
- No. 33. Izard. (xi, 81 p. mimeo., March 1942)
- No. 34. Jackson. (xv, 113 p. mimeo., October 1941)
- No. 44. Madison. (xvi, 70 p. mimeo., May 1942)
- No. 48. Monroe. (xv, 100 p. mimeo., April 1942)
- No. 49. Montgomery. (xvi, 64 p. mimeo., April 1942)
- No. 57. Polk. (xvii, 97 p. mimeo., January 1942)
- No. 62. Saline. (xv, 82 p. mimeo., May 1942)
- No. 63. Scott. (xi, 85 p. mimeo., March 1942)
- No. 65. Searcy. (x, 112 p. mimeo., June 1940)

## INVENTORIES OF COUNTY ARCHIVES (Cont'd)

CALIFORNIA, NORTHERN:  40-33756
    No. 1. Alameda, Vol II. (381 p., mimeo., February 1942)
    No. 10. Fresno. (vi, 624 p. mimeo., July 1940)
    No. 15. Kern. Vol. II. (v, 228 p. mimeo., June 1941)
    No. 22. Marin. (ii, 136 p. mimeo., December 1937)
    No. 27. Mono. (vi, 139 p. mimeo., April 1940)
    No. 29. Napa. (ii, 619 p. mimeo., March 1941)
    No. 36. San Benito. (vi, 585 p. mimeo., February 1940)
    No. 39. San Francisco. Vol. II. (vi, 418 p. mimeo., May 1940)
    No. 41. San Luis Obispo. (vi, 524 p. mimeo., November 1939)
    No. 42. San Mateo, (v, 184 p. mimeo., June 1938)
    No. 44. Santa Clara. (vi, 330 p. mimeo., April 1939)

CALIFORNIA, SOUTHERN:  40-33756
    No. 20. Los Angeles: Tax Collector's Office. (vi, 172 p. mimeo., January 1940)
        Assessor's Office. (viii, 228 p. mimeo., January 1941).
    No. 37. San Bernardino, Title-Line Inventory of. (v, 132 p. mimeo., August 1940)
    No. 38. San Diego: Vol. III. Tax and Financial Offices (vi, 238 p. mimeo., January 1941)
    No. 42. Santa Barbara, Title-Line Inventory of. (ii, 187 p. mimeo., January 1941)
    No. 57. Ventura, Title-Line Inventory of. (ii, 155 p. mimeo., August 1940)

COLORADO:  40-30844
    No. 2. Alamosa. (x, 13-112 pp. mimeo., June 1942)
    No. 3. Arapahoe. (v, 174 p. mimeo., February 1939)
    No. 6. Bent. (v, 175 p. mimeo., July 1938)
    No. 11. Conejos. (v, 179 p. mimeo., October 1938)
    No. 12. Costilla. (iv, 122 p. mimeo., May 1938)
    No. 22. Fremont. (iv, 146 p. mimeo., January 1938)
    No. 23. Garfield. (vi, 153 p. mimeo., June 1941)
    No. 27. Hinsdale. (v, 228 p. mimeo., October 1939)
    No. 35. Larimer. (v, 196 p. mimeo., October 1941)
    No. 38. Logan. (v, 292 p. mimeo., April 1940)
    No. 44. Morgan. (v, 291 p. mimeo., September 1939)
    No. 48. Phillips. (v, 292 p. mimeo., March 1941)
    No. 50. Prowers. (v, 139 p. mimeo., 1941)
    No. 57. San Miguel. (iv, 139 p. mimeo., January 1941)
    No. 61. Washington. (viii, 168 p. mimeo., April 1941)
    No. 63. Yuma. (v, 163 p. mimeo., February 1941)

DELAWARE:  42-4024
    No. 1. New Castle. (viii, 325 p. mimeo., 1941)

## INVENTORIES OF COUNTY ARCHIVES (Cont'd)

**FLORIDA:**          41-6030
- No. 8. Charlotte. (iv, 149 p. mimeo., November 1938)
- No. 10. Clay. (v, 478 p. mimeo., January 1941)
- No. 11. Collier. (vi, 134 p. mimeo., March 1938)
- No. 16. Duval. (v, 185 p. mimeo., February 1938)
- No. 18. Flagler. (v, 126 p. mimeo., August 1938)
- No. 25. Hardee. (v, 250 p. mimeo., June 1939)
- No. 26. Hendry. (v, 141 p. mimeo., June 1938)
- No. 37. Leon. (xiv, 201 p. mimeo., December 1941)
- No. 46. Okaloosa. (v, 179 p. mimeo., May 1939)
- No. 54. Pinellas. (v, 380 p. mimeo., June 1940)
- No. 58. Sarasota. (v, 217 p. mimeo., May 1939)
- No. 65. Wakulla. (xiii, 142 p. mimeo., March 1942)

**GEORGIA:**          40-13900
- No. 25. Chatham. (v, 160 p. mimeo., March 1938)
- No. 32. Clinch. (vii, 62 p. mimeo., September 1940)
- No. 37. Cook. (includes town archives within county) (xv, 114 p. mimeo., August 1941)
- No. 47. Dougherty. (x, 245 p. mimeo., January 1941)
- No. 50. Echols. (vii, 46 p. mimeo., September 1940)
- No. 81. Jefferson. (ix, 231 p. mimeo., May 1940)
- No. 88. Lee: Vol. I. Historical Sketch. (xi, 84 p. mimeo., April 1942)
      Vol. II. Records Entries. (xv, 97 p. mimeo., June 1942)
- No. 106. Muscogee. (x, 319 p. mimeo., January 1941)
- No. 121. Richmond. (v, 152 p.xx mimeo., April 1939)

**IDAHO:**          41-6031
County Government in Idaho: Supplementing Inventories of County Archives. (vii, 197 p. mimeo., June 1942)
- No. 6. Bingham. (iv, 216 p. mimeo., May 1942)
- No. 11. Boundary. (iv, 139 p. mimeo., February 1939)
- No. 17. Clark. (v, 115 p. mimeo., March 1940)
- No. 28. Kootenai. (v, 199 p. mimeo., October 1939)
- No. 30. Lemhi. (iii, 66 p. mimeo., May 1938)
- No. 34. Minidoka. (ii, 51 p. mimeo., September 1937)
- No. 35. Nez Perce. (v, 194 p. mimeo., June 1939)
- No. 39. Power. (v, 144 p. mimeo., April 1941)
- No. 41. Teton. (v, 123 p. mimeo., December 1940)

**ILLINOIS:**          39-26792
- No. 1. Adams. (vi, 210 p. mimeo., April 1939)
- No. 5. Brown. (iv, 93 p. mimeo., February 1938)
- No. 8. Carroll. (ii, 103 p. mimeo., December 1937)
- No. 10. Campaign. (xii, 118 p. printed January 1938)
- No. 12. Clark. (iv, 132 p. mimeo., June 1938)
- No. 18. Cumberland. (iv, 105 p. mimeo., April 1938)
- No. 20. Dewitt. (xiii, 324 p. mimeo., October 1941)
- No. 21. Douglas. (xiii, 282 p. mimeo., November 1939)
- No. 25. Effingham. (ix, 254 p. mimeo., September 1940)

## INVENTORIES OF COUNTY ARCHIVES (Cont'd)

**ILLINOIS** (Cont'd)  39-26792
- No. 26. Fayette. (xii, 165 p. plano., September 1939)
- No. 28. Franklin. (200 p. mimeo., January 1941)
- No. 39. Jackson. (vi, 206 p. mimeo., March 1939)
- No. 43. Jo Daviess. (ii, 122 p. mimeo., February 1938)
- No. 48. Knox. (v, 220 p. mimeo., September 1938)
- No. 53. Livingston. (x, 252 p. printed, June 1940)
- No. 54. Logan. (v, 207 p. mimeo., July 1938)
- Governmental Organization and Records System, Macon County, Illinois. (23 p. mimeo., December 1938)
- No. 56. Macoupin. (vii, 212 p. mimeo., July 1939)
- No. 65. Menard. (xii, 297 p. plano., April 1941)
- No. 68. Montgomery. (xi, 230 p. printed, October 1939)
- No. 69. Morgan. (vii, 213 p. mimeo., June 1939)
- No. 70. Moultrie. (277 p. mimeo., November 1941)
- No. 71. Ogle. (ix, 310 p. mimeo., August 1940)
- No. 72. Peoria. (xiv, 423 p. mimeo., January 1942)
- No. 74. Piatt. (ix, 266 p. mimeo., August 1940)
- No. 75. Pike. (iv, 121 p. mimeo., March 1938)
- No. 81. Rock Island. (xiii, 274 p. mimeo., December 1939)
- No. 82. Saline. (xii, 274 p. printed, February 1941)
- No. 83. Sangamon. (vii, 228 p. mimeo., April 1939)
- No. 85. Scott. (iv, 121 p. mimeo., May 1938)
- No. 86. Shelby. (xi, 236 p. printed, January 1940)
- No. 88. St. Clair. (ix, 345 p. mimeo., September 1939)
- No. 89. Stephenson. (iv, 143 p. mimeo., June 1938)
- No. 92. Vermilion. (x, 364 p. mimeo., March 1940)

**INDIANA:**  40-30847
- No. 2. Allen. (xiii, 380 p. multi., September 1939)
- No. 5. Blackford. (Prelim. edition, i, 76 p. mimeo., 1936)
- No. 6. Boone. (143 p. printed, 1937)
- No. 11. Clay. (xii, 404 p. multi., June 1939)
- No. 18. Delaware. (xiii, 387 p. mimeo., March 1940)
- No. 25. Fulton. (xii, 391 p. printed, May 1942)
- No. 28. Greene. (xii, 204 p. multi., October 1938)
- No. 34. Howard. (xii, 152 p. printed, September 1939)
- No. 38. Jay. (xii, 399 p. printed, July 1940)
- No. 46. La Porte. (xii, 189 p. printed, May 1939)
- No. 49. Marion. (xii, 219 p. printed, June 1938)
- No. 50. Marshall. (xii, 465 p. multi., June 1941)
- No. 53. Monroe. (xi, 433 p. multi., July 1940)
- No. 55. Morgan. (xi, 436 p. multi., February 1941)
- No. 65. Posey. (ix, 378 p. multi., June 1940)
- No. 71. St. Joseph. (xii, 248 p. printed, April 1939)
- No. 73. Shelby. (ix, 415 p. multi., July 1940)
- No. 79. Tippecanoe. (xii, 516 p. multi., August 1941)
- No. 80. Tipton. (xii, 404 p. multi., September 1941)
- No. 82. Vanderburgh. (xiv, 269 p. multi., February 1939)
- No. 87. Warrick. (xiv, 379 p. multi., January 1940)
- No. 90. Wells. (xii, 431 p. multi., September 1941)

## INVENTORIES OF COUNTY ARCHIVES (Cont'd)

**IOWA:**     40-33757
- No. 14. Carroll. (vii, 141 p. mimeo., July 1940)
- No. 18. Cherokee. (vi, 180 p. mimeo., May 1939)
- No. 25. Dallas. (v, 168 p. mimeo., August 1938)
- No. 31. Dubuque. (v, 172 p. mimeo., February 1938)
- No. 47. Ida. (v, 154 p. mimeo., May 1938)
- No. 50. Jasper. (v, 183 p. mimeo., December 1938)
- No. 69. Montgomery.(xiv, 132 p. mimeo., December 1941)
- No. 77. Polk. (xv, 208 p. mimeo., January 1942)
- No. 81. Sac. (viii, 164 p. mimeo., July 1940)
- No. 87. Taylor. (xiv, 131 p. mimeo., August 1941)
- No. 97. Woodbury.(viii, 371 p. mimeo., May 1940)

**KANSAS:**     40-31686
- No. 6. Bourbon. (vi, 423 p. mimeo., July 1940)
- No. 11. Cherokee.(vi, 334 p. mimeo., April 1940)
- No. 30. Franklin.(v, 249 p. mimeo., August 1939)
- No. 32. Gove. (xi, 172 p. mimeo., December 1941)
- No. 33. Graham. (v, 224 p. mimeo., December 1939)
- No. 35. Gray. (v, 269 p. mimeo., August 1939)
- No. 37. Greenwood. (v, 156 p. mimeo., May 1938)
- No. 46. Johnson. (ii, 115 p. mimeo., July 1937)
- No. 63. Montgomery. (v, 168 p. mimeo., September 1938)
- No. 64. Morris. (xv, 341 p. mimeo., June 1942)
- No. 70. Osage. (ix, 243 p. mimeo., April 1941)
- No. 74. Phillips.(ix, 208 p. mimeo., September 1941)
- No. 88. Seward. (v, 186 p. mimeo., December 1938)
- No. 89. Shawnee. (xi, 645 p. mimeo., December 1940)

**KENTUCKY:**     41-6032
- No. 3. Anderson. (ix, 379 p. mimeo., September 1941)
- No. 14. Breckenridge. (vi, 391 p. mimeo., September 1940)
- No. 20. Carlisle. (v, 166 p. mimeo., June 1938)
- No. 34. Fayette. (ii, 121 p. mimeo., August 1937)
- No. 57. Jessamine. (vi, 331 p. mimeo., February 1940)
- No. 61. Knox. (ii, 149 p. mimeo., December 1937)
- No. 63. Laurel. (ii, 244 p. mimeo., December 1938)
- No. 74. McCreary.(iii, 82 p. mimeo., February 1938)
- No. 82. Meade. (vi, 377 p. mimeo., January 1941)

**LOUISIANA:** (Parish Archives)     40-14734
Title-Line Inventory of the Parish Archives of Louisiana Parts 1 and 2, Acadia through Winn.((c) 300 p., December 1939)
- No. 2. Allen. (iv, 91 p. mimeo., June 1938)
- No. 4. Assumption. (xiii, 134 p. mimeo., March 1942)
- No. 6. Beauregard. (iv, 105 p. mimeo., October 1940)
- No. 8. Bossier. (v, 295 p. mimeo., August 1940)
- No. 10. Calcasieu.(iv, 113 p. mimeo., March 1938)
- No. 22. Grant. (iv, 110 p. mimeo., April 1940)
- No. 26. Jefferson.(iv, 437 p. mimeo., January 1940)
- No. 26. Jefferson. A Brief History. (Reprinted, in part from "A Brief History of Jefferson Parish," in Jefferson Parish Yearly Review, 1939, pp. 127-183;(iv, 25, v-ix p. mimeo., April 1940)

## INVENTORIES OF COUNTY ARCHIVES (Cont'd)

**LOUISIANA:** (Cont'd)
- No. 28. Lafayette. (iv, 118 p. mimeo., February 1938)
- No. 29. Lafourche. (xiii, 129 p. mimeo., March 1942)
- No. 34. Morehouse. (xii, 109 p. mimeo., March 1942)
- No. 35. Natchitoches. (v, 180 p. mimeo., September 1938)
- No. 36. Orleans: Preliminary Inventory of Notarial Records. (v, 172 p. mimeo., June 1939)
- No. 37. Ouachita. (xiii, 129 p. mimeo., March 1942)
- No. 38. Plaquemines. (iii, 228 p. mimeo., August 1939)
- No. 43. Sabine. (xiii, 145 p. mimeo., January 1942)
- No. 44. St. Bernard. (iii, 166 p. mimeo., December 1938)
- No. 45. St. Charles. (ii, 117 p. mimeo., November 1937)
- No. 55. Terrebonne. (xiii, 169 p. mimeo., May 1941)
- No. 59. Washington. (vi, 365 p. mimeo., March 1940)
- No. 60. Webster. (xiii, 141 p., mimeo., March 1942)

**MARYLAND:** 38-26211
- No. 1. Allegany. (iv, 101 p. mimeo., September 1937)
- No. 2. Anne Arundel. (ii, 353 p. mimeo., December 1941)
- No. 6. Carroll. (v, 273 p. mimeo., March 1940)
- No. 11. Garrett. (vi, 128 p. mimeo., June 1938)
- No. 13. Howard. (v, 181 mimeo., March 1939)
- No. 15. Montgomery. (v, 319 p. mimeo., February 1939)
- No. 21. Washington. (vi, 153 p. mimeo., December 1937)
- No. 22. Wicomico. (v, 222 p. mimeo., September 1940)

**MASSACHUSETTS:** 41-6033
- No. 5. Essex. (ii, 370 p. mimeo., December 1937)

**MICHIGAN:** 40-30848
- No. 2. Alger. (iii, 271 p. mimeo., March 1941)
- No. 4. Alpena. (iii, 72 p. mimeo., May 1938) Revised edition. (xiii, 261 p. mimeo., April 1942)
- No. 7. Baraga. (i, 46 p. mimeo., November 1937)
- No. 9. Bay. (ii, 339 p. mimeo., November 1940)
- No. 13. Calhoun. (v, 327 p. mimeo., May 1941)
- No. 16. Cheboygan. (iii, 115 p. mimeo., December 1938)
- No. 25. Genesee. (v, 224 p. printed, March 1940)
- No. 35. Iosco. (iii, 81 p. mimeo., May 1938)
- No. 36. Iron. (iv, 84 p. mimeo., June 1938)
- No. 38. Jackson. (iv, 360 p. mimeo., June 1941)
- No. 52. Marquette. (v, 297 p. mimeo., May 1940)
- No. 61. Muskegon. (xiii, 316 p. mimeo., December 1941)

**MINNESOTA:** 40-13902
- No. 1. Aitkin. (x, 172 p. mimeo., March 1942)
- No. 2. Anoka. (x, 135 p. mimeo., February 1942)
- No. 4. Beltrami. (x, 176 p. mimeo., November 1941)
- No. 5. Benton. (v, 293 p. mimeo., March 1940)
- No. 6. Big Stone. (x, 146 p. mimeo., August 1941)
- No. 7. Blue Earth. (iii, 76 p. mimeo., August 1937)

## INVENTORIES OF COUNTY ARCHIVES (Cont'd)

**MINNESOTA:** (Cont'd)
- No. 11. Cass. (x, 152 p. mimeo., February 1941)
- No. 12. Chippewa. (v, 177 p. mimeo., September 1940)
- No. 19. Dakota. (v, 158 p. mimeo., May 1940)
- No. 20. Dodge. (x, 122 p. mimeo., September 1941)
- No. 21. Douglas. (ix, 142 p. mimeo., March 1941)
- No. 22. Fairbault. (iv, 256 p. mimeo., October 1938)
- No. 23. Fillmore. (x, 156 p. mimeo., January 1942)
- No. 24. Freeborn. (iii, 91 p. mimeo., August 1937)
- No. 25. Goodhue. (x, 198 p. mimeo., August 1941)
- No. 26. Grant. (v, 301 p. mimeo., November 1939)
- No. 28. Houston. (x, 155 p. mimeo., December 1941)
- No. 29. Hubbard. (x, 157 p. mimeo., April 1941)
- No. 32. Jackson. (v, 329 p. mimeo., April 1940)
- No. 33. Kanabec. (x, 130 p. mimeo., May 1941).
- No. 41. Lincoln. (x, 119 p. mimeo., June 1941)
- No. 45. Marshall. (v, 308 p. mimeo., December 1939)
- No. 46. Martin. (v, 291 p. mimeo., October 1939)
- No. 47. Meeker. (x, 119 p. mimeo., November 1940)
- No. 48. Mille Lacs. (ix, 191 p. mimeo., February 1942)
- No. 49. Morrison. (v, 323 p. mimeo., April 1940)
- No. 51. Murray. (x, 143 p. mimeo., June 1941)
- No. 52. Nicollet. (iv, 195 p. mimeo., May 1938)
- No. 53. Nobles. (v, 273 p. mimeo., December 1939)
- No. 55. Olmsted. (v, 292 p. mimeo., April 1939)
- No. 56. Otter Tail. (xii, 184 p. mimeo., November 1940)
- No. 59. Pipestone. (v, 279 p. mimeo., August 1939)
- No. 64. Redwood. (ix, 139 p. mimeo., October 1941)
- No. 65. Renville. (x, 132 p. mimeo., December 1940)
- No. 66. Rice. (x, 128 p. mimeo., September 1940)
- No. 67. Rock. (v, 120 p. mimeo., September 1940)
- No. 70. Scott. (iv, 307 p. mimeo., January 1939)

Governmental Organization and Record System – 42-47838
Scott County, Minnesota (i, 48 p. mimeo., January 1939)
Reprinted from No. 70 Scott County.

- No. 71. Sherburne. (v, 172 p. mimeo., September 1940)
- No. 73. Stearns. (v, 171 p. mimeo., May 1940)
- No. 78. Traverse. (iv, 235 p. mimeo., October 1938)
- No. 79. Wabasha. (v, 326 p. mimeo., April 1939)
- No. 82. Washington. (iv, 284 p. mimeo., October 1938)
- No. 86. Wright. (v, 118 p. mimeo., September 1940)
- No. 87. Yellow Medicine. (x, 150 p. mimeo., October 1941)

**MISSISSIPPI:** 41-6035
- No. 3. Amite. (ii, 65 p. mimeo., September 1937)
- No. 18. Forrest. (v, 140 p. mimeo., June 1938)
- No. 22. Grenada. (v, 172 p. mimeo., April 1940)
- No. 27. Humphreys. (v, 180 p. mimeo., August 1941)
- No. 37. Lamar. (vi, 329 p. mimeo., July 1939)
- No. 55. Pearl River. (v, 127 p. mimeo., February 1938)
- No. 70. Tippah. Prelim. edition. (vi, 157 p. mimeo., June 1942)
- No. 72. Tunica. Prelim. edition. (viii, 184 p. mimeo., June 1942)
- No. 74. Walthall. Prelim. edition. (viii, 125 p. mimeo., June 1942)

## INVENTORIES OF COUNTY ARCHIVES (Cont'd)

**MISSOURI:** 40-13903
- No. 19. Cass. (vii, 142 p. mimeo., April 1941)
  Historical Sketch of Cass County, Missouri. (Reprinted from No. 19, Cass County. 15 p. mimeo., 1941)
- No. 26. Cole. (iv, 150 p. mimeo., November 1938)
- No. 30. Dallas. (v, 109 p. mimeo., November 1940)
- No. 42. Henry. (ix, 114 p. mimeo., October 1940)
  Historical Sketch of Henry County, Missouri. (Reprinted from No. 42. Henry County. 15 p. mimeo., October 1940)
- No. 51. Johnson. (xiv, 147 p. mimeo., October 1941)
- No. 58. Linn. (v, 144 p. mimeo., December 1938)
- No. 60. McDonald. (xii, 162 p. mimeo., February 1942)
- No. 61. Historical Sketch of Macon County. (18 p. August 1941)
- No. 64. Marion. (vii, 230 p. mimeo., January 1941) Historical Sketch of Marion County, Missouri. Reprinted from No. 64 Marion County. (iv, 32 p. mimeo., March 1941)
- No. 73. Jasper. (iv, 269 p. mimeo., January 1940) Historical Sketch of Jasper County, Missouri. (Reprinted from No. 73. Jasper County, 30 p. mimeo., 1941) Governmental Organization and Records System, Jasper County, Missouri. Reprinted from No. 73. Jasper County. (i, 66 p. mimeo., February 1940)
- No. 80. Pettis. (iv, 212 p. mimeo., June 1939)
- No. 82. Pike. (ii, 85 p. mimeo., November 1937)
- No. 90. Reynolds. (iv, 117 p. mimeo., June 1938)
- No. 91. Ripley. (iv, 92 p. mimeo., May 1938)
- No.102. Shelby. (iv, 168 p. mimeo., March 1939)

**MONTANA:** 40-30460
- No. 1. Beaverhead. (v, 203 p. mimeo., November 1939)
- No. 5. Carbon, Gallatin, Park, Stillwater, Sweet Grass. (xiv, 622 p. mimeo., Jan. 1942)
- No. 15. Flathead, Mineral, Lake, Ravalli, Lincoln, Sanders. (xv, 657 p. mimeo., November 1940)
- No. 16. Gallatin. (See No. 5.)
- No. 24. Lake. (See No. 15.)
- No. 27. Lincoln. (See No. 15.)
- No. 28. Madison. (vii, 208 p. mimeo., May 1940)
- No. 31. Mineral. (See No. 15.)
- No. 32. Missoula. (v, 190 p. mimeo., September 1938)
- No. 34. Park. (See No. 5.)
- No. 41. Ravalli. (See No. 15.)
- No. 45. Sanders. (See No. 15.)
- No. 47. Silver Bow. (v, 231 p. mimeo., July 1939)
- No. 48. Stillwater. (See No. 5.)
- No. 49. Sweet Grass. (See No. 5.)
- No. 51. Toole. (v, 123 p. mimeo., October 1938)

**NEBRASKA:** 40-30849
- No. 37. Gosper. (ii, 174 p. mimeo., June 1940)
- No. 39. Greeley. (vii, 211 p. mimeo., May 1941)
- No. 47. Howard. (vii, 211 p. mimeo., December 1941)
- No. 58. Loup. (vi, 127 p. mimeo., May 1941)
- No. 61. Merrick. (xi, 147 p. mimeo., February 1942)
- No. 80. Seward. (v, 216 p. mimeo., June 1939)
- No. 91. Webster. (x, 157 p. mimeo., March 1942)

## INVENTORIES OF COUNTY ARCHIVES (Cont'd)

**NEVADA:**                                                                 40-30850
   No. 3. Douglas.   (ii, 72 p. mimeo., November 1937)
   No. 4. Elko.      (v, 178 p. mimeo., December 1938)
   No. 6. Eureka.    (v, 201 p. mimeo., October 1939)
   No. 11. Mineral.  (iii, 195 p. mimeo., March 1941)
   No. 12. Nye.      (iii, 216 p. mimeo., September 1940)
   No. 13. Ormsby.   (iii, 178 p. mimeo., March 1940)
   No. 16. Washoe.   (v, 115 p. mimeo., September 1938)

**NEW HAMPSHIRE:**                                                          38-26704
   No. 1. Belnap.    (ii, 64 p. mimeo., June 1938)
   No. 2. Carroll.   (iv, 160 p. mimeo., February 1939)
   No. 3. Cheshire.  (iv, 196 p. mimeo., August 1939)
   No. 4. Coos.      (iv, 238 p. mimeo., February 1940)
   No. 5. Grafton.   (v, 152 p. mimeo., April 1940)
   No. 7. Merrimack. Prelim. edition. (iii, 25 p. mimeo., December 1936)

**NEW JERSEY:**                                                             40-30851
   No. 2. Bergen.    (vii, 279 p. printed, 1939)
   No. 14. Morris. Prelim. edition. (iii, 135 p. printed September 1937)
   No. 15. Ocean.    (x, 179 p. mimeo., August 1940)
   No. 16. Passaic.  (x, 228 p. mimeo., January 1940)

**NEW MEXICO:**                                                             38-28883
   No. 1. Bernalillo. (v, 255 p. mimeo., September 1938)
   No. 4. Colfax.    (iii, 94 p. mimeo., November 1937)
   No. 7. Dona Ana.  (xvi, 261 p. mimeo., November 1940)
   No. 8. Eddy.      (vi, 213 p. mimeo., May 1939)
   No. 9. Grant.     (xvi, 344 p. mimeo., December 1941)
   No. 12. Hidalgo.  (xiv, 192 p. mimeo., 1941)
   No. 15. Luna.     (xvi, 306 p. mimeo., April 1942)
   No. 17. Mora.     (xiv, 282 p. mimeo., November 1941)
   No. 18. Otero.    (v, 202 p. mimeo., October 1939)
   No. 23. Sandoval. (vi, 150 p. mimeo., January 1939)
   No. 24. San Miguel. (xvi, 266 p. mimeo., February 1941)
   No. 26. Sierra.   (xvi, 272 p. mimeo., June 1942)
   No. 29. Torrance. (vi, 181 p. mimeo., April 1939)
   No. 30. Union.    (v, 202 p. mimeo., June 1940)
   No. 31. Valencia. (vi, 236 p. mimeo., July 1940)

**NEW YORK STATE:**                                                         38-26212
   No. 1. Albany.    (iv, 170 p. mimeo., October 1937)
   No. 3. Broome.    (vi, 87 p. mimeo., July 1938)
   No. 4. Cattaraugus. (v, 84 p. mimeo., February 1939)
   No. 6. Chautauqua. (v, 85 p. mimeo., October 1938)
   No. 7. Chemung.   (v, 84 p. mimeo., January 1939)
   No. 51. Ulster. Part II. (xxvii, 434 p. mimeo., October 1940)

## INVENTORIES OF COUNTY ARCHIVES (Cont'd)

**NEW YORK CITY:**     40-31687
- No. 1. Bronx    (vi, 336 p. mimeo., February 1940)
- No. 2. Kings.    (vii, 371 p. mimeo., January 1942)
- No. 5. Richmond Borough and County. (viii, 411 p. mimeo., August 1939)

**NORTH CAROLINA:**     38-28119 Rev.
- Vol. 1. Alamance through Columbus. (26 counties, xi, 491 p. printed, March 1938)
- Vol. 2. Craven through Moore. (40 counties, xi, 568 p. printed, August 1938)
- Vol. 3. Nash through Yancey. (37 counties, x, 760 p. printed, October 1939)

**NORTH DAKOTA:**     41-6036
- No. 17. Golden Valley. (vi, 114 p. mimeo., July 1941)
- No. 29. Mercer. (vi, 125 p. mimeo., March 1941)
- No. 53. Williams. (iv, 119 p. mimeo., April 1938)

**OHIO:**     37-26502
- No. 1. Adams. (vi, 237 p. mimeo., December 1938)
- No. 2. Allen. (ii, 114 p. mimeo., December 1936)
- No. 3. Ashland. ( p. mimeo., 1942)
- No. 5. Athens. (vi, 275 p. mimeo., May 1939)
- No. 8. Brown. (vi, 204 p. mimeo., June 1938)
- No. 15. Columbiana. (x, 302 p. mimeo., July 1942)
- No. 18. Cuyahoga. Vol. 1. (xxv, 347 p. mimeo., April 1937)
- No. 24. Fayette. (v, 297 p. mimeo., July 1940)
- No. 25. Franklin. (x, 528 p. mimeo., May 1942)
- No. 28. Geuga. (x, 323 p. mimeo., Aug. 1942)
- No. 31. Hamilton. (iv, 311 p. mimeo., October 1937)
- No. 32. Hancock. (x, 356 p. mimeo., December 1941)
- No. 40. Jackson. (ix, 269 p. mimeo., January 1942)
- No. 42. Knox. (vi, 308 p. mimeo., April 1939)
- No. 43. Lake. (ix, 273 p. mimeo., October 1941)
- No. 47. Lorain. (x, 376 p. mimeo., 1941)
- No. 48. Lucas. (ii, 148 p. mimeo., April 1937)
- No. 49. Madison. (ix, 263 p. mimeo., August 1941)
- No. 57. Montgomery. (x, 345 p. mimeo., December 1941)
- No. 66. Pike. (ix, 296 p. mimeo., May 1942)
- No. 71. Ross. (vi, 307 p. mimeo., June 1939)
- No. 73. Scioto. (vi, 236 p. mimeo., August 1938)
- No. 74. Seneca. (ix, 343 p. mimeo., April 1942)
- No. 76. Stark. (vi, 345 p. mimeo., January 1940)
- No. 77. Summit. (x, 322 p. mimeo., May 1941)
- No. 78. Trumbull. (iii, 128 p. mimeo., April 1937)
- No. 84. Washington. (viii, 330 p. mimeo., April 1938)

**OKLAHOMA:**     40-14735
- No. 3. Atoka. (vii, 125 p. mimeo., February 1941)
- No. 5. Beckham. (v, 238 p. mimeo., March 1939)
- No. 11. Cherokee. (x, 156 p. mimeo., August 1941)
- No. 13. Cimarron. (vi, 104 p. mimeo., January 1938)
- No. 31. Haskell. (viii, 113 p. mimeo., July 1940)

## INVENTORIES OF COUNTY ARCHIVES (Cont'd)

**OKLAHOMA** (Cont'd)
- No. 41. Lincoln. Prelim. edition. (v, 128 p. mimeo., January 1940)
- No. 46. McIntosh. (v, 183 p. mimeo., June 1938)
- No. 49. Mayes. (iii, 127 p. mimeo., May 1937)
- No. 51. Muskogee. (iv, 181 p. mimeo., December 1937)
- No. 61. Pittsburg. (viii, 182 p. mimeo., May 1940)
- No. 64. Pushmataha. (v, 173 p. mimeo., May 1938)

**OREGON:** 40-13905
- No. 2. Benton. (viii, 344 p. mimeo., April 1942)
- No. 4. Clatsop. (v, 273 p. mimeo., September 1940)
- No. 6. Coos. (viii, 323 p. mimeo., May 1942)
- No. 14. Hood River. (v, 203 p. mimeo., December 1939)
- No. 17. Josephine. (v, 192 p. mimeo., November 1939)
  - Essay of County Governmental Organization in Oregon. (Reprinted from No. 17. Josephine County. December 1939)
- No. 18. Klamath. (iii, 340 p. mimeo., October 1941)
- No. 22. Linn. (v, 181 p. mimeo., May 1939)
- No. 25. Morrow. (v, 57 p. mimeo., October 1937.)
- No. 26. Multnomah, Vol. I. (v, 222 p. mimeo., June 1940)
  - Vol. II. (v, 218 p. mimeo., May 1940)
  - Governmental Organization, Multnomah County. An Abstract from No. 26. Multnomah County. Vol. I. (82 p. mimeo., May 1940)
  - Historical Sketch and Governmental organization, Multnomah County, Oregon. (A reprint from No. 26. Multnomah County, Vol. I. (ii, 83 p. mimeo., March 1941)
- No. 29. Tillamook. (v, 240 p. mimeo., April 1940)
  - History, Governmental Organization and Records System of Tillamook County. (Reprint from No. 29. Tillamook County) (79 p. mimeo., September 1940)
- No. 30. Umatilla. (ix, 373 p. mimeo., January 1942)
- No. 33. Wasco. (v, 332 p. mimeo., February 1941)
- No. 34. Washington. (v, 300 p. mimeo., November 1940)

**PENNSYLVANIA:** 40-14736
County Government and Archives in Pennsylvania. (xi, 533 p. printed, 1942)
- No. 1. Adams. (vi, 313 p. offset, August 1941)
- No. 4. Beaver. (xvi, 408 p. printed, April 1942)
- No. 6. Berks. (iii, 409 p. offset, August 1941)
- No. 7. Blair. (vi, 294 p. offset, May 1941)
- No. 8. Bradford. (p. printed 1942)
- No. 23. Delaware. (v, 254 p. mimeo., August 1939.)
  - Revised edition. (Offset, vi, 287 p. October 1941)
- No. 25. Erie. (vi, 374 p. offset, August 1940)
- No. 26. Fayette. (viii, 291 p. offset, May 1940)
- No. 27. Forest. (vi, 201 p. offset, October 1940)

INVENTORIES OF COUNTY ARCHIVES (Cont'd)

PENNSYLVANIA (Cont'd)
- No. 30. Greene. (vi, 259 p. offset, November 1940)
- No. 36. Lancaster. (vi, 294 p. offset, February 1941)
- No. 37. Lawrence. (xvi, 392 p. printed, January 1942)
- No. 40. Luzerne. (x, 239 mimeo., December 1938)
- No. 62. Warren. (xiii, 343 p. printed, February 1942)
- No. 63. Washington. (400 p. offset, May 1941)
- No. 64. Wayne. (vi, 207 p. mimeo., July 1939)
- No. 65. Westmoreland. (xiv, 459 p. printed January 1942)

SOUTH CAROLINA: 38-26571
- No. 1. Abbeville. (iv, 106 p. mimeo., April 1938)
- No. 2. Aiken. (iv, 115 p. mimeo., December 1938)
- No. 3. Allendale. (v, 64 p. mimeo., August 1938)
- No. 4. Anderson. (v, 169 p. mimeo., August 1939)
- No. 11. Cherokee. (vi, 176 p. mimeo., February 1941)
- No. 17. Dillon. (iv, 78 p. mimeo., December 1938)
- No. 21. Florence. (iv, 106 p. mimeo., August 1938)
- No. 27. Jasper. (iv, 72 p. mimeo., October 1938)
- No. 31. Lee. (ii, 46 p. mimeo., January 1937)
- No. 35. McCormick. (vi, 135 p. mimeo., June 1940)
- No. 37. Oconee. (v, 133 p. mimeo., June 1939)
- No. 39. Pickens. (xii, 257 p. mimeo., June 1941)
- No. 40. Richland. (vi, 239 p. mimeo., April 1940)
- No. 41. Saluda. (vi, 168 p. mimeo., October 1940)

SOUTH DAKOTA: 42-19824
- No. 3. Bennett. (v, 89 p. mimeo., October 1940)
- No. 8. Buffalo. (i, 42 p. mimeo., December 1937)
- No. 12. Clark. (ix, 132 p. mimeo., March 1941)
- No. 24. Faulk. (vii, 129 p. mimeo., April 1942)
- No. 27. Haakon. (viii, 106 p. mimeo., January 1941)
- No. 35. Jackson and Washabaugh. (ix, 162 p. mimeo., November 1941)
- No. 47. Millette. (iii, 86 p. mimeo., December 1940)
- No. 48. Miner. (viii, 133 p. mimeo., July 1941)
- No. 65. Washabaugh. (see No. 35)

TENNESSEE: 40-31689
- No. 1. Anderson. (v, 89 p. mimeo., July 1941)
- No. 2. Bedford. (vi, 152 p. mimeo., May 1940)
- No. 5. Blount. (v, 89 p. mimeo., April 1941)
- No. 6. Bradley. (vi, 137 p. mimeo., January 1941)
- No. 11. Cheatham. (x, 158 p. mimeo., November 1941)
- No. 17. Crockett. (v, 115 p. mimeo., August 1940)
- No. 33. Hamilton. (iv, 130 p. mimeo., November 1937)
- No. 38. Haywood. (v, 161 p. mimeo., March 1939)
- No. 53. Loudon. (v, 128 p. mimeo., March 1941)

## INVENTORIES OF COUNTY ARCHIVES (Cont'd)

**TENNESSEE** (Cont'd)
- No. 75. Rutherford. (vi, 138 p. mimeo., March 1938)
- No. 82. Sullivan. (xv, 220 p. mimeo., March 1942)
- No. 84. Tipton. (v, 166 p. mimeo., July 1941)
- No. 95. Wilson. (v, 177 p. mimeo., September 1938)

**TEXAS:** 40-13906
- No. 10. Bandera. (iii, 113 p. mimeo., June 1940)
- No. 11. Bastrop. (viii, 128 p. mimeo., June 1941)
- No. 25. Brown. (iii, 147 p. mimeo., May 1940)
- No. 28. Caldwell. (xii, 119 p. mimeo., November 1941)
- No. 29. Calhoun. (viii, 115 p. mimeo., January 1941)
- No. 61. Denton. (iii, 125 p. mimeo., August 1937)
- No. 62. De Witt. (iv, 123 p. mimeo., January 1940)
- No. 75. Fayette. (v, 167 p. mimeo., December 1940)
- No. 86. Gillespie. (xii, 149 p. mimeo., October 1941)
- No. 92. Gregg. (iii, 179 p. mimeo., August 1940)
- No. 94. Guadalupe. (v, 303 p. mimeo., December 1939)
- No. 105. Hays. (iv, 105 p. mimeo., January 1940)
- No. 111. Hood. (iii, 69 p. mimeo., March 1940)
- No. 120. Jackson. (viii, 103 p. mimeo., December 1940)
- No. 158. Marion. (iii, 118 p. mimeo., March 1940)
- No. 166. Milam. (viii, 131 p. mimeo., June 1941)
- No. 167. Mills. (iii, 78 p. mimeo., April 1940)
- No. 181. Orange. (xii, 181 p. mimeo., December 1941)
- No. 198. Robertson. (viii, 140 p. mimeo., March 1941)
- No. 199. Rockwall. (iv, 73 p. mimeo., February 1940)
- No. 202. Sabine. (iv, 217 p. mimeo., June 1939)
- No. 213. Somervell. (iii, 63 p. mimeo., March 1940)
- No. 232. Uvalde. (viii, 143 p. mimeo., May 1941)
- No. 247. Wilson. (100 p. mimeo., November 1939)

**UTAH:** 40-33759
- No. 2. Box Elder. (iv, 160 p. mimeo., December 1938). Historical Sketch and Governmental Organization of Box Elder County. (Reprinted from No. 2, Box Elder County. (25 p. mimeo., February 1939)
- No. 4. Carbon. (v, 261 p. mimeo., July 1940)
- No. 5. Daggett. (iv, 133 p. mimeo., August 1939)
- No. 8. Emery. (viii, 179 p. mimeo., March 1941)
- No. 10. Grand. (v, 89 p. mimeo., April 1938)
- No. 15. Morgan. (ii, 39 p. mimeo., August 1937)
- No. 20. Sanpete. (vii, 271 p. multi., October 1941)
- No. 23. Tooele. (iv, 259 p. mimeo., June 1939)
- No. 24. Uintah. (v, 254 p. mimeo., November 1940)
- No. 25. Utah. (ii, 329 p. mimeo., September 1940)
- No. 26. Wasatch. (iv, 95 p. mimeo., July 1938)
- No. 29. Weber. (Prelim. edition, iv, 236 p. mimeo., January 1940)

**VERMONT:**
- Vol. 7. Lamoille. (Prelim. edition, 32 p. mimeo., December 1936)

## INVENTORIES OF COUNTY ARCHIVES (Cont'd)

**VIRGINIA:** 41-6037
- No. 4. Amelia. (viii, 251 p. mimeo., February 1940)
- No. 13. Brunswick. (xii, 256 p. mimeo., January 1943)
- No. 21. Chesterfield. (viii, 299 p. printed, August 1938)
- No. 27. Dinwiddie. (v, 207 p. mimeo., July 1939)
- No. 47. Isle of Wight. (ix, 289 p. mimeo., April 1940)
- No. 60. Middlesex. (x, 147 p. mimeo., May 1939)
- No. 73. Powhatan. (v, 202 p. mimeo., August 1939)
- No. 75. Prince George. (xiii, 276 p. mimeo., October 1941)
- No. 88. Southampton. (viii, 265 p. mimeo., March 1940)

**WASHINGTON:** 39-29180
- No. 1. Adams. (v, 275 p. mimeo., June 1939)
- No. 2. Asotin. (v, 209 p. mimeo., December 1938)
- No. 3. Benton. (v, 258 p. mimeo., June 1939)
- No. 4. Chelan. (xvi, 229 p. mimeo., April 1942)
- No. 8. Cowlitz. (xvi, 323 p. mimeo., September 1942)
- No. 12. Garfield. (x, 139 p. mimeo., November 1941)
- No. 17. King. Part 2. Judicial Officers.
  (viii, 112 p. mimeo., August 1941)
- No. 21. Lewis. (vi, 346 p. mimeo., April 1940)
- No. 22. Lincoln. (xiii, 246 p. mimeo., January 1942)
- No. 26. Pend Oreille. (ii, 82 p. mimeo., September 1937)
- No. 29. Skagit. (iii, 133 p. mimeo., March 1938)
- No. 31. Snohomish. Historical Sketch and Government Organization and Records System. Prelim. edition.
  (vii, 153 p. mimeo., March 1942)
- No. 32. Spokane. (x, 620 p. mimeo., March 1941)
- No. 33. Stevens. (xiii, 259 p. mimeo., February 1942)
- No. 39. Yakima. (vi, 435 p. mimeo., July 1940)

**WEST VIRGINIA:** 41-52395
- No. 11. Gilmer. (xv, 120 p. mimeo., March 1942)
- No. 12. Grant. (ii, 127 p. mimeo., May 1938)
- No. 22. Lincoln. (ii, 136 p. mimeo., March 1938)
- No. 24. Marion. (v, 310 p. mimeo., February 1941)
- No. 28. Mineral. (v, 120 p. mimeo., January 1941)
- No. 31. Monroe. (v, 200 p. mimeo., November 1938)
- No. 36. Pendleton. (v, 201 p. mimeo., January 1939)
- No. 38. Pocahontas. (ii, 112 p. mimeo., December 1937)
- No. 40. Putnam. (xiii, 125 p. mimeo., April 1941)
- No. 42. Randolph. (v, 179 p. mimeo., November 1938)
- No. 43. Ritchie. (ii, 160 p. mimeo., September 1938)
- No. 44. Roane. (xiii, 109 p. mimeo., August 1941)
- No. 46. Taylor. (v, 173 p. mimeo., April 1939)

## INVENTORIES OF COUNTY ARCHIVES (Cont'd)

**WISCONSIN:**            41-52396
    County Government in Wisconsin:        42-20943
        Vol. I. (xxxvii, 263 p. mimeo., 1942)
        Vol. II. (xxxvii, 264-529 p. mimeo., 1942)
        Vol. III. (xxxvii, 530-765 p. mimeo., 1942)
    No. 3. Barron. (iv, 387 p. mimeo., March 1939)
    No. 6. Buffalo. (v, 277 p. mimeo., September 1940)
    No. 9. Chippewa. (xi, 204 p. mimeo., April 1941)
    No. 10. Clark. (ix, 164 p. mimeo., July 1941)
    No. 16. Douglas. (xiv, 242 p. mimeo., 1942)
    No. 17. Dunn. (viii, 168 p. mimeo., June 1941)
    No. 18. Eau Claire. (xiii, 175 p. mimeo., January 1942)
    No. 22. Grant. (xiv, 182 p. mimeo., 1942)
    No. 27. Jackson. (xii, 170 p. mimeo., November 1941)
    No. 32. La Crosse. (iv, 324 p. mimeo., June 1939)
    No. 37. Marathon. (v, 387 p. mimeo., August 1940)
    No. 41. Monroe. (xi, 184 p. mimeo., February 1941)
    No. 43. Oneida. (xi, 231 p. mimeo., April 1941)
    No. 46. Pepin. (ix, 148 p. mimeo., August 1941)
    No. 48. Polk. (xiii, 193 p. mimeo., 1941)

**WYOMING:**            41-6038
    No. 8. Goshen. (iv, 178 p. mimeo., June 1940)
    No. 11. Laramie. (ii, 115 p. mimeo., July 1938)
    No. 12. Lincoln. (vii, 166 p. mimeo., May 1941)
    No. 15. Park. (vi, 99 p. mimeo., January 1942)
    No. 16. Platte. (v, 172 p. mimeo., December 1939)
    No. 19. Sweetwater. (v, 171 p. mimeo., March 1939)

## INVENTORIES OF MUNICIPAL AND TOWN ARCHIVES

CONNECTICUT:      40-30845
- No. 1. Fairfield County:
  - Vol. XXI. Weston. (iv, 108 p. mimeo., May 1940)

- No. 2. Hartford County:
  - Vol. I. Avon, Berlin, Bloomfield. (iv, 299 p. mimeo., July 1939)
  - Vol. XVII. Newington. (iv, 98 p. mimeo., December 1939)

- No. 5. New Haven County:
  - Vol. VIII. North Branford, North Haven, Orange, Oxford, Prospect, Seymour, Southbury. (iv, 189 p. mimeo., December 1938)

DISTRICT OF COLUMBIA:      40-38332
Board of Accountancy, Board of Examiners and Registrars of Architects, Board of Barber Examiners, Board of Cosmetology. (Prelim. edition, vii, 31 p. mimeo., April 1940)

FLORIDA:
A List of Municipal Corporations in Florida. (79 p. mimeo., June 1939)      39-26981

A List of Municipal Corporations in Florida. Revised. (89 p. mimeo., March 1941)      41-17285

GEORGIA:
- No. 37. Cook County:
  - Adel, Cecil, Lenox, Sparks. (78-96 p. in Inventory of County Archives of Georgia)

INDIANA:
Municipal Government in Indiana. Vol. III., Third Class Cities:
Part A. Master Essays. (viii, 381 p. mimeo., March 1942)

Part B. Kokomo. (vi, 141 p. mimeo., March 1942)

LOUISIANA:
Franklinton. (X, 54 p. mimeo., April 1941)      42-2479

Thibodaux. (115 p. mimeo., March 1942)

MAINE:      41-7033
Town Government in Maine, Prelim. edition. Designed for use with Inventories of Town Archives. (ii, 206 p. mimeo., April 1940)      40-26963

- No. 4. Franklin County:
  - Vols. I & II. Avon and Berlin. (v, 104 p. mimeo., May 1939)
  - Vol. IV. Chesterville. (iii, 77 p. mimeo., June 1939)
  - Vol. V. & VI. Coplin, Dallas. (iv, 74 p. mimeo., 1939)

INVENTORIES OF MUNICIPAL AND TOWN ARCHIVES (Cont'd)

MAINE: (Cont'd)
    No. 4. Franklin County: (Cont'd)
        Vol. VII. Eustis. (iv, 75 p. mimeo., 1939)

    No. 5. Hancock County:
        Vol. I. Towns of Mt. Desert: Mount Desert, Bar Harbor, Cranberry Isles, Seaville, Tremont, Southwest Harbor. (iv, 236 p. mimeo., March 1939).

        Vol. I-a. Index to Vol. I. Towns of Mt. Desert. (iii, 66 p. mimeo., March 1940)

    No. 11. Piscataquis County:
        Vol. VI. Brownville. (vi, 92 p. mimeo., November 1940)

MARYLAND:
    No. 1. Allegany County:
        Barton, Cumberland, Frostburg, Lonaconing, Luke, Midland. (77-86 p. in Inventory of County Archives of Maryland)

    No. 2. Anne Arundel County:
        Annapolis, Arundel-on-the-Bay. (277-307 p. in Inventory of County Archives of Maryland).

    No. 6. Carroll County:
        Hamstead, Manchester, Mt. Airy, New Winsor, Sykesville, Taneytown, Union Bridge, Westminster. (203-252 p. in Inventory of County Archives of Maryland)

    No. 11. Garrett County:
        Accident, Dear Park, Friendsville, Grantsville, Kitzmillersville, Loch Lynn, Mountain Luke Park, Oakland. (91-105 p. in Inventory of County Archives of Maryland)

    No. 13. Howard County:
        Ellicott City. (153-155 p. in Inventory of County Archives of Maryland)

    No. 15. Montgomery County:
        Barnesville, Brooksville, Chevy Chase, Gaithersburg, Garrett Park, Glen Echo, Kensington, Laytonville, Poolesville, Rockville, Somerset, Takoma Park, Washington Grove. (246-287 p. in Inventory of County Archives of Maryland)

    No. 21. Washington County:
        Boonsboro, Clearspring, Funkstown, Hagerstown, Hancock, Keedysville, Sharpsburg, Smithburg, Williamsport, (101-132 p. in Inventory of County Archives in Maryland)

    No. 22. Wicomico County:
        Delmar, Hebron, Mardela Springs, Salisbury, Sharpstown, Willards. (160-205 p. in Inventory of County Archives in Maryland)

## INVENTORIES OF MUNICIPAL AND TOWN ARCHIVES (Cont'd)

**MASSACHUSETTS:**

No. 2. Berkshire County:
    Vol. XXII. Pittsfield. Part I. (ix, 166 p. multi., 1942)
                        Part II. (xii, 269 p. multi., 1942)

No. 6. Franklin County:
    Vol. I. Ashfield. (iii, 108 p. mimeo., 1940)
        A Sketch of the History and Government of Ashfield, (Reprinted from Vol. I., Ashfield, 48 p. mimeo., 1941)

    Vol. II. Bernardston. (93 p. mimeo., 1941)

    Vol. III. Buckland. (ii, 78 p. mimeo., 1940)
        A Sketch of the History and Government of Buckland. (Reprinted from Vol. III, Buckland, ii, 36 p. mimeo., 1940)

    **Vol. XXIV.** Warwick. (ix, 86 p. mimeo., 1942)

No. 7. Hampden County:
    Vol. I. Agawam. (iii, 74 p. mimeo., 1941)

    Vol. V. Chicopee. (xi, 296 p. multi., October 1939)

    Vol. VIII. Hampden. (iv, 97 p. mimeo., 1941)

No. 8. Middlesex County:
    Vol. IV. Ashland. (Part I. History of the Town of, (141 p. printed 1942)      42-24814

    Vol. V. Ayer. (iii, 148 p. multi., 1941)

    Vol. XXIX. Maynard. (iv, 146 p. multi., 1941)

No. 11. Norfolk County:
    Vol. I. Avon. (ii, 83 p. multi., 1941)

    Vol. II. Bellingham. (ii, 75 p. multi., August 1939)

    A Brief History of the Town of Braintree in Massachusetts, 1640-1940. (64 p. printed, 1940)

    Vol. IV. Brookline. (iii, 348 p. multi., 1940)
        A Sketch of the History and Government of Brookline. (Reprinted from Vol. IV, Brookline; iv, 69 p. multi., 1940)

## INVENTORIES OF MUNICIPAL AND TOWN ARCHIVES (Cont'd)

**MASSACHUSETTS:** (Cont'd)

- No. 11. Norfolk County: (Cont'd)
  Vol. XI. Holbrook. (v, 179 p. multi., 1941)
  A Sketch of the History and Government of Holbrook.
  (Reprinted from Vol. XI. Holbrook, 54 p. multi., 1941)

- No. 13. Suffolk County:
  Vol. I. Boston. Part 5. (v, 349 p. multi., February 1940)
  Part 9. (vii, 286 p. multi., 1942)

- No. 14. Worcester County:
  Vol. II. Athol. (iii, 231 p. multi., 1941)

  Vol. III. Auburn. (iii, 99 p. mimeo., February 1940)

  Vol. IV. Barre. (ii, 132 p. mimeo., 1940)
  A Sketch of the History and Government of Barre.
  (Reprinted from Vol. IV, Barre; ii, 45 p. mimeo., 1940)

  Vol. V. Berlin. (iii, 108 p. mimeo., 1941)

  Vol. XI. Clinton. (iii, 117 p. multi., 1941)

**MICHIGAN:**

- No. 82. Wayne County:     41-8034
  City of Detroit:
  No. 15. City Treasurer. (vi, 72 p. mimeo., December 1940)

  No. 31. Arts Commission. (vi, 38 p. mimeo., March 1941)

  No. 32. Department of Recreation. (viii, 49 p. mimeo., December 1940)

  Detroit Recorders Court. (ix, 61 p. mimeo., June 1942)

  City of Hamtramck:
  Office of Engineer. (Prelim. inventory; v, 36 p. mimeo., May 1940)

  City of Muskegon:
  List of the City Offices of the City of Muskegon. (iv, 36 p. mimeo., July 1941)

## INVENTORIES OF MUNICIPAL AND TOWN ARCHIVES (Cont'd)

NEW HAMPSHIRE:            40-13904
    Town Government in New Hampshire. (iii, 151 p. mimeo.,
        July 1940)         40-28601

    No. 1. Belknap County:
        Vol. VIII. New Hampton. (ii, 84 p. mimeo., April 1941)

        Vol. IX. Sanbornton. (ii, 90 p. mimeo., October 1941)

    No. 6. Hillsboro County:
        Vol. III. Bedford. (ii, 75 p. mimeo., January 1942)

    No. 7. Merrimack County:
        Vol. VI. Canterbury. (v, 79 p. mimeo., February 1941)

    No. 8. Rockingham County:
        Vol. I. Atkinson. (iv, 67 p. mimeo., October 1939)

        Vol. II. Auburn. (iv, 77 p. mimeo., December 1939)

        Vol. IV. Candia. (iv, 81 p. mimeo., August 1940)

        Vol. V. Chester. (v, 83 p. mimeo., May 1940)

        Vol. XI. Exeter. (ii, 98 p. mimeo., December 1940)

        Vol. XIII. Greenland. (iv, 80 p. mimeo., July 1941)

NEW JERSEY:
    No. 7. Essex County:            40-35280
        Vol. XVII. Orange. (xiii, 202 p. printed, May 1941)

    No. 9. Hudson County:
        Vol. II. East Newark. (xi, 106 p. printed, May 1941)

    No.13. Monmouth County:
        Vol. VII. Belmar. (ix, 120 p. printed March 1942)

    No.14. Morris County:
        Vol. VIII. Denville. (xiii, 150 p. printed, May 1941)

        Vol. XXXVIII. Wharton. (x, 65 p. printed 1939)

NEW YORK CITY:
    No. 1. Bronx Borough. (xii, 302 p. offset, 1942)

    No. 5. Richmond Borough. (see Inventory of County Archives
        of New York City.

INVENTORIES OF MUNICIPAL AND TOWN ARCHIVES (Cont'd)

OHIO: 40-35281
    No. 18. Cuyahoga County:
        Vol. V. Cleveland, Records. (xxxii, 538 p. multi., December 1939)

        Vol. VI. Cleveland, Department of Public Safety. (xxv, 495 p. multi., October 1941)

        Vol. VII. Cleveland, Department of Health and Welfare. (xxix, 506 p. multi., December 1941)

        Guide to Records of Cuyahoga County Municipalities other than Cleveland: Vol. 2. Muncipal Archives. (cv, 669 p., mimeo., December 1938)

RHODE ISLAND:
    No. 2. Kent County:
        Vol. IV. West Greenwich. (viii, 80 p. mimeo., April 1942)

    No. 4. Providence County:
        Vol. X. North Providence. (viii, 159 p. mimeo., February 1942)

TEXAS:
An Inventory of the Colonial Archives of Texas:

    No. 3. Municipality of Brazoria, 1832-37. (iii, 120 p. mimeo., June 1940)

UTAH:
    A History of Ogden. Preprint of the Inventory of the Municipal Archives of Utah. (77 p, printed, October 1940)     40-28741

VERMONT: 40-13907
    No. 1. Addison County:
        Vol. II. Bridport. (iv, 60 p. mimeo., 1939)

    No. 4. Chittenden County:
        Vol. I. Bolton. (iv, 56 p. mimeo., May 1939)

        Vol. III. Charlotte. (iv, 72 p. mimeo., 1939)

        Vol. V. Essex. (iv, 102 p. mimeo., August 1940)

    No. 6. Franklin County:
        Vol. IV. Fairfax. (iv, 73 p. mimeo., 1940)

    No. 7. Grand Isle County:
    Alburgh, Grand Isle, Isle LaMotte, North Hero, South Hero, Two Heroes, Alburgh Village. (iii, 259 p. mimeo., December 1939)

## INVENTORIES OF MUNICIPAL AND TOWN ARCHIVES (Cont'd)

**VERMONT:** (Cont'd)

No. 8. Lamoille County:
- Vol. I. Belvidere. (iv, 58 p. mimeo., October 1940)
- Vol. II. Cambridge. (iii, 96 p. mimeo., June 1941)
- Vol. III. Eden. (iv, 58 p. mimeo., December 1940)
- Vol. IV. Elmore. (iv, 62 p. mimeo., February 1941)
- Vol. V. Hyde Park. (iv, 76 p. mimeo., December 1940)
- Vol. VI. Johnson. (iv, 88 p. mimeo., July 1941)
- Vol. VII. Morristown and Sterling Village of Morrisville. (iv, 121 p. mimeo., 1940)
- Vol. VIII. Stowe and Mansfield. (iv, 130 p. mimeo., 1940)
- Vol. IX. Waterville. (iv, 53 p. mimeo., July 1939)
- Vol. X. Walcott. (iv, 68 p. mimeo., October 1939)

No. 10. Oreans County:
- Vol. I. Albany. (iv, 75 p. mimeo., 1940)
- Vol. V. Coventry. (iv, 64 p. mimeo., August 1940)
- Vol. VII. Derby, Villages of Derby, Derby Line. (iv, 103 p. mimeo., 1939)
- Vol. VII. Derby, Supplement: Town of Salem 1781-1880. (ii, 40 p. mimeo., April 1841)

No. 11. Rutland County:
- Vol. I. Benson (ii, 62 p. mimeo., April 1941)
- Vol. III. Castleton. (iv, 104 p. mimeo., March 1941)
- Vol. VI. Dandy. (86 p. mimeo., October 1941)
- Vol. VIII. Hubbardton. (iv, 56 p. mimeo., November 1940)
- Vol. XIII. Mt. Tabor. (iii, 60 p. mimeo., March 1941)
- Vol. XXII. Shrewsbury. (iv, 59 p. mimeo., 1940)

INVENTORIES OF MUNICIPAL AND TOWN ARCHIVES (Cont'd)

VERMONT: (Cont'd)
    No. 11. Rutland County: (Cont'd)
        Vol. XXIV. Tinmouth. (v, 64 p. mimeo., December 1941)

        Vol. XXV. Wallingford. (ii, 87 p. mimeo., April 1940)

    No. 13. Windham County:
        Vol. III. Brookline. (76 p. mimeo., 1939)

        Vol. VI. Grafton. (iv, 74 p. mimeo., January 1941)

        Vol. IX. Jamaica. (iv, 74 p. mimeo., January 1941)

    No. 14. Windsor County:
        Vol. VI. Cavendish. (iv, 100 p. mimeo., January 1941)

        Vol. XII. Plymouth. (iv, 65 p. mimeo., 1940)

WISCONSIN:
    Municipal and Town Government in Wisconsin. (ix, 213 p. 1942)

    Third Class Cities:
        Cudahy. (x, 270 p. mimeo., December 1941)        42-16942 Rev.
        Wauwatosa. (x, 271 p. mimeo., 1942)

    No. 141. Greendale. (x, 87 p. mimeo., November 1941)        42-14202

## TRANSCRIPTIONS OF PUBLIC ARCHIVES

**FLORIDA:**
    Transcriptions of Public Archives in Florida: Ordinances      42-19892
        and Minutes of the City of St. Augustine, Vol. I.
        1821-1827; Vol. III. 1843-1861. (180 p. mimeo.,
        November 1941)

**LOUISIANA:**
    Transcriptions of Parish Records of Louisiana:      39-26978
        No. 24. Iberville Parish: Series I. Police Jury Minutes.
            Vol. 1. 1850-1862. (xlviii, 188 p. mimeo., April 1940)
            Vol. 2. 1880-1901. (lxxvii, 361 p. mimeo., May 1940)
            Vol. 3. 1901-1916. (lxxxi, 468 p. mimeo., July 1940)
            Vol. 4. 1916-1925. (l, 281 p. mimeo., March 1941)
            Vol. 5. 1925-1936. (cviii, 613 p. mimeo., March 1941)
            General Index, 1850-1936. (xxix, 284 p. mimeo.,
            March 1942)

        No. 26. Jefferson Parish: Series I. Police Jury Minutes.
            Vol. 1. 1834-1843. (xxxvii, 237 p. mimeo., June 1939)
            Vol. 3. 1858-1870. (lix, 319 p. mimeo., November 1939)
            Vol. 3-A. 1871-1884. (lix, 347 p. mimeo., January 1940)
            Vol. 4. 1870-1879. (lxix, 370 p. mimeo., March 1940)
            Vol. 5. 1879-1888. (lxvi, 386 p. mimeo., April 1940)
            Vol. 6. 1889-1895. (lxiv, 400 p. mimeo., April 1940)
            Vol. 7. 1895-1904. (liii, 480 p. mimeo., June 1940)
            Vol. 8. 1905-1912. (lvii, 342 p. mimeo., July 1940)
            Vol. 9. 1912-1918. (lv, 492 p. mimeo., September 1940)
            Vol.10. 1918-1924. (lxxx, 532 p. mimeo., September 1940)
            Vol.11. 1924-1929. (lxxxv, 650 p. mimeo., September 1940)
            Vol.12. 1930-1935. (lxiv, 622 p. mimeo., November 1940)
            Vol.13. 1935-1938. (xlix, 545 p. mimeo., February 1941)

        No. 44. St. Bernard Parish: Series I. Police Jury Minutes.
            Vol. 1. 1870-1877. (xl, 107 p. mimeo., July 1941)
            Vol. 2. 1880-1895. (xlix, 342 p. mimeo., August 1941)
            Vol. 3. 1895-1914. (xlv. 383 p. mimeo., October 1941)
            Vol. 4. 1914-1922. (xxxv, 217 p. mimeo., December 1941)
            Vol. 5. 1922-1929. (lxiii, 497 p. mimeo., February 1942)
            Vol. 6. 1929-1940. (lxi, 501 p. mimeo., March 1942)

**MICHIGAN:**      42-8542
    Transcriptions of Municipal Archives of Michigan:
        Minutes of Meetings of the Charter Commission of the
            City of Hamtramck, October 19, 1921 - April 5,
            1922. (vii, 47 p. mimeo., April 1940)

        Minutes of the Meetings of the Village Council of      40-28831
            Hamtramck. August 29, 1901 - July 26, 1905.
            (vi, 357, vii-xxiv p. mimeo., May 1940)
            1907-1908. (vi, 211 p. mimeo., September 1941)

TRANSCRIPTIONS OF PUBLIC ARCHIVES (Cont'd)

MICHIGAN: (Cont'd).
    Minutes of the Meetings of the Townships of Bucklin, Pepin and Dearborn, May 28, 1827 - April 1857. (viii, 147 p. mimeo., April 1941)    41-26045

    Minutes of the Meetings of the Township of Springwells, April 17, 1861 - March 4, 1872. (v, 188 p. mimeo., August 1941)    42-8543

MISSISSIPPI:
    No. 2. Adams County:
        Vol. 1. Minutes of the Court of General Quarter Sessions of the Peace, 1799-1801. (xxii, 107 p. mimeo., July 1942)

        Vol. 2. Minutes of the County Court, 1802-1804. (xxvi, 131 p. mimeo., July 1942)

MISSOURI:
    Minutes of the St. Louis Board of Trustees, 1808-1809. (v, 6 p. mimeo., December 1940)

NEW JERSEY:
    Transcriptions of Early County Records of New Jersey;
    Gloucester County Series:
        Revolutionary War Documents. (xvi, 144 p. mimeo., August 1940)    40-28791 Rev.

        Slave Documents. (xiii, 66 p. mimeo., August 1940)

NEW YORK STATE:
    Transcriptions of Early County Records of New York State:    40-26220
    Minutes of the Board of Supervisors of Ulster County, 1710/1 to 1730/1. (xvi, 61 p. mimeo., December 1939)

    Records of the Road Commissioners of Ulster County:
        Vol. 1. 1722-1769. (xx, 111 p. mimeo., May 1940)

        Vol. 2. 1769-1795. (vi, 175 p. mimeo., November 1940)

NEW YORK CITY:
    Transcriptions of Early Town Records of New York:    40-29275 Rev.
    Town Minutes of Newtown:
        Vol. 1. 1656-1688. Town Clerk's Office, Newtown, Queens County, N. Y. (xx, 209 p. mimeo., June 1940)

        Vol. 2. 1653-1734. Town Clerk's Office, Newtown, Queens County, N. Y.
        Part I. (xvii, 314 p. mimeo., February 1941)

        Part II. (iv, 315-628 p. mimeo., February 1941)

## TRANSCRIPTIONS OF PUBLIC ARCHIVES (Cont'd)

NEW YORK CITY: (Cont'd)

    Minutes of the Town Courts of Newtown, 1656-1690. (ix, 314 p. mimeo., August, 1940)     42-13575

    The Earliest Volume of Staten Island Records, 1678-1813. (xliv, 172 p. mimeo., March 1942)     42-18983

TENNESSEE:

Transcription of the County Archives of Tennessee:

    Minutes of the County Court of Shelby County:     41-24441
        Book I. 1820-1824. (iv, 100 p. mimeo., January 1941)

    Minutes of the County Court of Knox County:     43-1173
        Book O. 1792-1795. (v, 277 (15) p. mimeo., March 1941)

WISCONSIN:

Wisconsin Territorial Papers: County Series:

    Crawford County; Proceedings of the County Board of Supervisors, November 29, 1821 - November 19, 1850. (iv, 311 p. mimeo., 1942)

    Iowa County:     42-16348

        Vol. 1. Proceedings of the County Board of Supervisors, 1830-1843. (iv, 275 p. mimeo., 1942)

        Vol. 2. Proceedings of the County Board of Supervisors, 1843-1850. (iv, 281 p. mimeo., 1942)

        Vol. 3. Index to the Proceedings of the County Board of Supervisors, 1830-1850. (v, 51 p. mimeo., 1942)

    St. Croix County; Proceedings of the County Board of Supervisors, October 5, 1840 - April 2, 1849. (v, 116 p. mimeo., 1941)     41-46396

## VITAL STATISTICS

**ALABAMA:**
    Guide to Public Vital Statistics Records in Alabama: Preliminary
        Edition. (vi, 73 p. mimeo., March 1942)     42-19821

    Guide to Vital Statistics Records in Alabama: Church Archives.
        (xi, 327 p. mimeo., May 1942)     42-24202

**ARIZONA:**
    The 1864 Census of the Territory of Arizona. (viii, 210 p.
        mimeo., November 1938)     39-26345

    Guide to Public Vital Statistics Records in Arizona. (vii,
        62 p. mimeo., August 1941)     42-13638 Rev.

**ARKANSAS:**
    Guide to Vital Statistics Records in Arkansas: Church Archives.
        (xv, 620 p. mimeo., April 1942)     42-19822

**COLORADO:**
    Guide to Vital Statistics in Colorado:     42-20517
        Vol. I. Public Archives. (147 p. mimeo., 1942)

        Vol. II. Church Archives. (166 p. mimeo., 1942)

**CALIFORNIA:**
    Guide to Public Vital Statistics Records in California:     42-13641 Rev.
        Vol. I. Birth Records. (ii, 72 p. mimeo., June 1941)

        Vol. II. Death Records. (ii, 62 p. mimeo., July 1941)

    Guide to Church Vital Statistics Records in California:     42-24200
        Alameda and San Francisco Counties; Six Denominations.
        (iv, 63 p. mimeo., May 1942)

**FLORIDA:**
    Guide to Public Vital Statistics Records in Florida. (iii,
        70 p. mimeo., February 1941)     41-52713 Rev.

    Guide to Supplementary Vital Statistics from Church Records
        in Florida; Preliminary Edition.
        Vol. I. Alachu. (xii, 330 p. mimeo., June 1942)

        Vol. II. Gilchrist. (xii, 331-646 p. mimeo., June 1942)

        Vol. III. Orange. (xii, 647-981 p. mimeo., June 1942)

**GEORGIA:**
    Guide to Public Vital Statistics Records in Georgia. (v, 73 p.
        mimeo., June 1941)

**IDAHO:**
    Guide to Public Vital Statistics Records in Idaho:
        State and County (iv, 47 p. mimeo., March 1942)     42-16408

## Vital Statistics (Cont'd)

**ILLINOIS:**

    Guide to Public Vital Statistics Records in Illinois.
        (vii, 137 p. mimeo., May 1941)                     41-50890

    Guide to Church Vital Statistics Records in Illinois.
        (Preliminary edition) (xxii, 359 p. mimeo.,
        February 1942)                                         42-24201

**INDIANA:**

    Guide to Public Vital Statistics Records in Indiana.
        (v, 265 p. mimeo., July 1941)                     43-1174

**IOWA:**

    Guide to Public Vital Statistics Records in Iowa. (vi,
        113 p. mimeo., October 1941)

**KANSAS:**

    Guide to Public Vital Statistics Records in Kansas.
        (viii, 262 p. mimeo., March 1942)               42-19823

**KENTUCKY:**

    Guide to Public Vital Statistics Records in Kentucky.
        (xxix, 257 p. mimeo., February 1942)

**LOUISIANA:**

    Guide to Public Vital Statistics Records in Louisiana
        (51 p. mimeo., December 1942)

    Guide to Vital Statistics Records of Church Archives in
        Louisiana.
        Vol. I. Protestant and Jewish Churches
        (173 p. mimeo., December 1942)

    Guide to Vital Statistics Records of Church Archives in
        Louisiana.
        Vol. II. Roman Catholic Churches (27 p. mimeo.,
        December 1942).

**MASSACHUSETTS:**

    Guide to Public Vital Statistics Records in Massachusetts.
        (vi, 342 p. mimeo., 1942)                       42-20516

**MICHIGAN:**

    Vital Statistics Holdings by Government Agencies in
        Michigan:
        Birth Records. (v, 166 p. mimeo., 1941)         41-26558

        Marriage Records. (iv, 77 p. mimeo., 1941)      42-1464

        Death Records. (vi, 209 p. mimeo., July 1942)

        Divorce Records. (vi, 56 p. mimeo., May 1942)

    Guide to Church Vital Statistics Records in Michigan:
        Wayne County. (vii, 151 p. mimeo., April 1942)

## Vital Statistics (Cont'd)

**MINNESOTA:**

    Guide to Public Vital Statistics Records in Minnesota.
        (vi, 142 p. mimeo., 1941)                                     42-17762

    Guide to Church Vital Statistics Records in Minnesota:
        Baptisms, Marriages, and Funerals. (iv, 253 p.
        mimeo., April 1942)                                       42-19637

**MISSISSIPPI:**

    Guide to Vital Statistics Records in Mississippi:
        Vol. I. Public Archives. (v, 62 p. mimeo., April 1942)    42-14378

        Vol. II. Church Archives. (iv, 702 p. mimeo., July 1942)

**MISSOURI:**

    Guide to Public Vital Statistics: Records in Missouri.
        (v, 120 p. mimeo., July 1941)                             42-14378

    Guide to Vital Statistics: Church Records in Missouri.
        (ii, 236 p. mimeo., April 1942)

**MONTANA:**

    Guide to Public Vital Statistics Records in Montana.
        (viii, 85 p. mimeo., March 1941)                         41-26559

    Inventory of the Vital Statistics Records of Churches and
        Religious Organizations in Montana. Preliminary
        Edition. (iv, 117 p. mimeo., July 1942)               43-1026

**NEBRASKA:**

    Guide to Public Vital Statistics Records in Nebraska.
        (ii, 94 p. mimeo., September 1941)                     42-15484

**NEVADA:**

    Guide to Public Vital Statistics Records in Nevada.
        (vi, 26 p. mimeo., December 1941)                     42-14376

**NEW HAMPSHIRE:**

    Guide to Public Vital Statistics Records in New Hampshire.

    Guide to Church Vital Statistics Records in New Hampshire
        Preliminary Edition. (viii, 104 p. mimeo., May 1942)     42-19636

**NEW JERSEY:**

    Guide to Vital Statistics Records in New Jersey.
        Vol. I. Public Archives. (313 p. mimeo., June 1941)     42-14379

        Vol. II. Church Archives. (vii, 588 p. mimeo., 1942)

    Guide to Naturalization Records in New Jersey. (vii, 185 p.
        mimeo., December 1941)

## Vital Statistics (Cont'd)

NEW MEXICO:
    Guide to Public Vital Statistics Records in New Mexico.
        (ix, 135 p. mimeo., March 1942)     42-15171

NEW YORK:
    Guide to Public Vital Statistics Records in New York State
        (Inclusive of New York City):
        Vol. I. Birth Records. (xviii, 260 p. mimeo.,
        January 1942)     42-14331

        Vol. II. Marriage Records. (xiv, 277 p. mimeo.,
        August 1942)

        Vol. III. Death Records. (viii, 263 p. mimeo., 1942)

    Guide to Vital Statistics Records of Churches in New York     42-20127
        State (exclusive of New York City)

        Vol. I. (xvi, 442 p. mimeo., May 1942)

        Vol. II. (xvi, 506 p. mimeo., June 1942)

    Guide to Vital Statistics Records in the City of New York:
        Churches:
            Borough of Bronx. (xiv, 26 p. mimeo., April 1942)

            Borough of Queens. (vi, 39 p. mimeo., May 1942)

            Borough of Richmond. (iv, 21 p. mimeo., 1942)

            Borough of Manhattan. (vi, 73 p. mimeo., 1942)

            Borough of Brooklyn. (v, 67 p. mimeo., 1942)

NORTH CAROLINA:
    Guide to Vital Statistics Records in North Carolina:
        Vol. I. Public Vital Statistics: (iv, 62 p. mimeo.,
        June 1942)

NORTH DAKOTA:
    Guide to Public Vital Statistics Records in North Dakota.     42-17212
        (iv, 77 p. mimeo., August 1941)

    Guide to Church Vital Statistics Records in North Dakota.
        (150 p. mimeo., March 1942)     42-18019

OKLAHOMA:
    Guide to Public Vital Statistics Records in Oklahoma.
        (vii, 85 p. mimeo., June 1941)     41-52361

OREGON:
    Guide to Public Vital Statistics Records in Oregon.     42-18931
        (xi, 80 p. mimeo., April 1942)

## Vital Statistics (Cont'd)

**RHODE ISLAND:**

    Summary of Legislation Concerning Vital Statistics in Rhode Island. (18 p. mimeo., July 1937)      39-26191

    Guide to Public Vital Statistics Records: Births, Marriages, Deaths in State of Rhode Island and Providence Plantations. (xiv, 280 p. mimeo., October 1941)      42-15271

    Guide to Church Vital Statistics Records in the State of Rhode Island and Providence Plantations (vi, 172 p. mimeo., June 1941)

**SOUTH DAKOTA:**

    Guide to Public Vital Statistics Records in South Dakota. (viii, 82 p. mimeo., January 1942)      42-18676

**TENNESSEE:**

    Guide to Public Vital Statistics Records in Tennessee. (iv, 146 p. mimeo., June 1941)      41-52966

    Guide to Church Vital Statistics Records in Tennessee. (vii, 510 p. mimeo., August 1942)

**TEXAS:**

    Guide to Public Vital Statistics Records in Texas. (177 p. mimeo., June 1941)

**UTAH:**

    Census of Weber County (exclusive of Green River Precinct) Provisional State of Desoret, 1850. (ii, 21 p. mimeo., October 1937)

    Guide to Public Vital Statistics Records in Utah. (ii, 54 p. multi., November 1941)

**VIRGINIA:**

    Guide to the Manuscript Collections of the Virginia Baptist Historical Society.
        Supplement No. 1. Index to the Obituary Notices in the Religious Herald, Richmond, Virginia, 1828-1938. (iv, 386 p. mimeo., December 1940)      41-52314

        Supplement No. 2. Index to Marriage Notices in the Religious Herald, Richmond, Virginia, 1828-1938.
        Vol. I. A-L. (iv, 371 p. mimeo., August 1941)

        Vol. II. M-Z. (v, 316 p. mimeo., September 1941)

    Index to Marriage Notices in the Southern Churchman, 1835-1941:
        Vol. A-K. (ix, 316 p. mimeo., May 1942)

        Vol. L-Z. (ix, 323 p. mimeo., May 1942)

## Vital Statistics (Cont'd)

**WASHINGTON:**

    Guide to Public Statistics Records in Washington. (v, 131 p. mimeo., June 1941)      42-1467

    Guide to Church Vital Statistics Records in Washington. Preliminary Edition. (vii, 93 p. mimeo., February 1942)      42-15487

**WEST VIRGINIA:**

    Inventory of Public Vital Statistics Records in West Virginia: Births, Deaths and Marriages. (iv, 75 p. mimeo., March 1941)      41-52707 Rev.

    Guide to Church Vital Statistics Records in West Virginia. (xviii, 278 p. mimeo., February 1942)      42-15487

**WISCONSIN:**

    Guide to Public Vital Statistics Records in Wisconsin. (ix, 274 p. mimeo., September 1941)      42-1468

    Guide to Church Vital Statistics Records in Wisconsin. (xiii, 257 p. mimeo., February 1942)      42-14606

    Outline of Vital Statistics Laws in Wisconsin. (xvii, 140 p. mimeo., September 1941)      42-7394

**WYOMING:**

    Guide to Public Vital Statistics in Wyoming. (iii, 31 p. mimeo., June 1941)      42-14377

    Guide to Vital Statistics Records in Wyoming: Church Archives. Preliminary Edition. (62 p. mimeo., March 1942)

## CHURCH ARCHIVES PUBLICATIONS

ALABAMA:
    Inventory of the Church Archives of Alabama:
        Protestant Episcopal Church  (iv, 106 p. mimeo.,
        November 1939)      40-26268 Rev.

ARKANSAS:
    Inventory of the Church of Arkansas:
        Church of Christ Scientist. (iii, 35. mimeo.,
        October 1941)

COLORADO:
    Inventory of the Church and Synogogue Archives of
        Colorado:
        Jewish. (iv, 34 p. mimeo., May 1941)      42-25335 Rev.

CONNECTICUT:
    Inventory of the Church Archives of Connecticut:
        Lutheran. (iii, 187 p. mimeo., March 1941)      41-13949

        Protestant Episcopal. (iv, 309 p. mimeo.,
        September 1940)      40-28948

DELAWARE:
    Inventory of the Church Archives of Delaware:
        Preprint of Section 22. Lutheran Church and 29.
        Protestant Episcopal (iv, 43 p. mimeo., June 1938)      42-29551

DISTRICT OF COLUMBIA:
    Inventory of the Church Archives of the District of
        Columbia:
        Protestant Episcopal Church, Diocese of Washington:
        Vol. 1. (xi, 382 p. mimeo., December 1940)      40-28474 Rev.

            Vol. 2. Washington Cathedral. (Prelim. edition,
            iv, 122 p. mimeo., April 1940)
        (Roman Catholic Church) Preprint of Inventory of St.
        Patrick's Church and School. (23 p. mimeo.,
        August 1941)      42-13911

FLORIDA:
    Inventory of the Church Archives of Florida;
        Baptist Bodies:      40-30846 Rev.
        No. 3. Black Creek Baptist Association
            (iv, 20 p. mimeo., July 1940)

        No. 12. Lake County Baptist Association. (iv, 33 p.
            mimeo., April 1940)

        No. 17. Northeast Florida Baptist Association (iv,
            21 p. mimeo., April 1940)

## CHURCH ARCHIVES PUBLICATIONS (Cont'd)

**FLORIDA:** (Cont'd)
    Inventory of the Church Archives of Florida: Baptist Bodies: Cont'd.
        No. 18. Northwest Coast Baptist Association.
            (iv, 25 p. mimeo., October 1940)

        No. 19. Okaloosa Baptist Association.
            (iv, 21 p. mimeo., May 1940)

        No. 20. Orange Blossom Baptist Association.
            (iv, 40 p. mimeo., May 1940)

        No. 21. Palm Lake Baptist Association. (iv, 16 p. mimeo., July 1940)

        No. 25. Pinellas County Baptist Association. (iv, 28 p. mimeo., June 1940)

        No. 30. Seminole Baptist Association. (iv, 42 p. mimeo., June 1940)

        No. 32. Southwest Baptist Association. (iv, 29 p. mimeo., September 1939)

        Florida State Association of Old Line Baptist Composed of Missionary Baptist Churches. (v, 14 p. mimeo., July 1940)     41-12629

    Translation and Transcription of Church Archives of Florida, Roman Catholic Records:
        St. Augustine Parish, White Baptisms, 1784-1792. (viii, 162 p. mimeo., March 1941)     41-20194

**GEORGIA:**
    Inventory of the Church and Synagogue Archives of Georgia:
        Atlanta Association of Baptist Churches. (v, 92 p. mimeo., April 1941)     41-13950

        Fairburn Missionary Baptist Association (v, 82 p. mimeo., September 1941)     42-13904

**ILLINOIS:**
    Inventory of the Church Archives of Illinois:
        Presbytery of Cairo. (x, 76 p. mimeo., November 1941)

        Presbytery of Springfield. (xii, 117 p. mimeo., January 1942)     42-15892

        Cumberland Presbyterian Church. (xiii, 165 p. mimeo., February 1942)     42-24071

**LOUISIANA:**
    Inventory of the Church and Synagogue Archives of Louisiana:
        Jewish Congregations and Organizations. (xvii, 183 p. mimeo., October 1941)     42-13639

## CHURCH ARCHIVES PUBLICATIONS (Cont'd)

MARYLAND:
    Inventory of the Church Archives of Maryland:
        Protestant Episcopal Church. Diocese of Maryland.
            (v, 310 p. mimeo., November 1940)         41-14069

MASSACHUSETTS:
    Inventory of the Church Archives of Massachusetts:
        Universalist Churches. (iii, 489 p. mimeo., 1942)         42-17650

MICHIGAN:
    Inventory of the Church and Synagogue Archives of Michigan:
        African Methodist Episcopal Church: Michigan
            Conference. (v, 24 p. mimeo., September 1940)         41-23360

        Church of the Nazarene: Michigan District Assembly:
            (vii, 50 p. mimeo., April 1942)         42-19638

        Churches of God: Michigan Assemblies. (iv, 62 p.
            mimeo., May 1941)         42-13928

        Dearborn Churches. (v, 54 p. mimeo., August 1940)         41-23364

        Evangelical and Reformed Church. (45 p. mimeo.,
            April 1941)         41-13951

        Evangelical Church, Michigan Conference. (v, 58 p.
            mimeo., March 1941)         41-13952

        Jewish Bodies. (vi, 65 p. mimeo., March 1940)

        Pilgrim Holiness Church: Michigan District. (vii,
            27 p. mimeo., April 1942)

        Presbyterian Church in the U. S. A.:
            Presbytery of Detroit. (v, 64 p. mimeo.,
            August 1940)         41-23362

            Presbytery of Flint. (iii, 30 p. mimeo.,
            October 1941)         41-46397

        Protestant Episcopal Church:
            Diocese of Michigan. (v, 126 p. mimeo.,
            March 1940)

            Diocese of Northern Michigan. (v, 41 p. mimeo.,
            1940)         40-28930

            Diocese of Western Michigan. (v, 46 p. mimeo.,
            June 1940)         41-23363

CHURCH ARCHIVES PUBLICATIONS (Cont'd)
    Inventory of the Church and Synagogue Archives of
        Michigan: (Cont'd)

        Roman Catholic Church:
            Diocese of Detroit (v, 186 p. mimeo., July 1941)     41-23361

        Salvation Army in Michigan. (viii, 49 p. mimeo.,
            April 1942)

MISSISSIPPI:
    Inventory of the Church and Synagogue Archives of Mississippi:

        Jewish Congregations and Organizations. (v, 41 p.
            mimeo., November 1940)                              41-12017

        Protestant Episcopal Church, Diocese of Mississippi.
            (vii, 146 p. mimeo., June 1940)                     40-28973 Rev.

MISSOURI:
    Inventory of the Church Archives of Missouri: Baptist Bodies,
        No. 1. Tebo Baptist Association (vii, 55 p. mimeo.,
        December 1940)                                          42-18304

    Transcriptions:
        Bethel Church Book. Minutes of the Proceedings of the
            Bethel Church 1806-1867. (iv, 82 p. mimeo.,
            November 1940)                                      40-28827

        Bethel Church Minutes. (Reprinted from Records of
            Proceedings of the Bethel Church. (iii, 7 p.
            mimeo., November 1940)                              41-24705

NEVADA:
    Inventory of the Church Archives of Nevada:
        Protestant Episcopal Church. (vi, 69 p. mimeo.,
            January 1941)                                       41-27400

        Roman Catholic Church. (v, 49 p. mimeo., August 1939)   39-29218 Rev.

NEW HAMPSHIRE:
    Inventory of the Church Archives of New Hampshire:
        Protestant Episcopal Church

        Roman Catholic Church. (ii, 127 p. mimeo. April 1938)   38-26413

NEW JERSEY:
    Inventory of the Church Archives of New Jersey:
        Baha'i Assemblies (26 p. mimeo., December 1940)         41-20125

        Baptist Bodies (xxii, 289 p. mimeo., December 1938)     39-26433 Rev.

        Baptist Bodies: Seventh Day Baptist Supplement
            (161 p. mimeo., August 1939)                        39-26433 Rev.

CHURCH ARCHIVES PUBLICATIONS (Cont'd)
    Inventory of the Church Archives of New Jersey: (Cont'd)

        Christian Reformed. (39 p. mimeo., February 1941)

        Congregational Christian. (99 p. mimeo., March 1941)         41-23365

        Evangelical Church. (37 p. mimeo., May 1941)                 42-1015

        Presbyterian Churches. (562 p. mimeo., August 1940)          41-24696

        Protestant Episcopal Churches: Diocese of New Jersey
            and Diocese of Newark. (434 p. mimeo., February
            1940)                                                    41-12018

        Salvation Army: Jersey City. (34 p. mimeo., April
            1940)                                                    41-12019

        Society of Friends

        Unitarian Church. (ii, 32 p. mimeo., June 1940)              41-19467

    Transcriptions of Early Church Records of New Jersey:

        Colporteur Reports to the American Tract Society,
            1841-1846. (iv, 123 p. mimeo., July 1940)                40-28789 Rev.

        John Brainerd's Journal (1761-1762) Presbyterian.
            (iii, 35 p. mimeo., May 1941)                            42-20955

NEW YORK STATE:
    Inventory of the Church Archives of New York State:

        Protestant Episcopal Church:
        Diocese of Western New York. (xxvi, 69, xxvii-xl p.
            mimeo., May 1939)                                        39-26979 Rev.

        Diocese of Rochester. (xiii, 266 p. mimeo., June
            1941)                                                    41-20126

NEW YORK CITY:
    Inventory of the Church Archives of New York City:

        Eastern Orthodox Churches and the Armenian Apostolic
            Church in America. (xxvii, 178 p. mimeo.,
            December 1940 -                                          41-23472

        Lutheran Church. (xii, 152 p. mimeo., December 1940)         41-13952

        Methodist Church. (xv, 216 p. mimeo., December 1940)         41-14071

        Presbyterian Church in the United States of America.
            (viii, 160 p. mimeo., March 1940)

## CHURCH ARCHIVES PUBLICATIONS (Cont'd)

Inventory of the Church Archives of New York City (Cont'd)

Protestant Episcopal Church,
Diocese of Long Island, Vol. 2, Brooklyn
and Queens. (x, 67 p. mimeo., September 1940)  40-28967

Diocese of New York, Vol. 2, Manhattan, Bronx
and Richmond. (xi, 153 p. mimeo., December 1940)

Reformed Church in America (ix, 95 p. mimeo., Aug. 1939)

Roman Catholic Church; Archdiocese of New York,
Vol. 2, The Bronx, Manhattan and Richmond. (x, 181 p.
mimeo., July 1941)

Society of Friends. (i, 224 p. mimeo., 1940)  41-22471

### NORTH CAROLINA:
Inventory of the Church Archives of North Carolina:

Southern Baptist Convention:
Allegany Association (vi, 12 p. mimeo., March 1940)  40-30852 Rev.

Brunswick Association. (vi, 23 p. mimeo., January 1941)  41-13954

Central Association. (vi, 40 p. mimeo., February 1941)  41-13955

Flat River Association. (vi, 39 p. mimeo. February 1941)  41-13956

Raleigh Association. (vi, 56 p. mimeo., July 1940)  41-52391

Stanley Association. (vi, 33 p. mimeo., February 1941)  41-13957

Yancey Association. (iv, 43 p. mimeo., February 1942)  42-17651

### OHIO:
Roman Catholic Church; Parishes of the Catholic Church,
Diocese of Cleveland (447 p. printed, September 1942)

### OKLAHOMA:
Inventory of the Church Archives of Oklahoma:
No. 7. Bryan County, (iii, 24 p. mimeo., October 1937)

### PENNSYLVANIA:
Inventory of the Church and Synagogue Archives of Pennsylvania:
Society of Friends. (iii, 397 p. offset, December 1941)  42-14607

## CHURCH ARCHIVES PUBLICATIONS (Cont'd)

RHODE ISLAND:
    Inventory of the Church Archives of Rhode Island:

        Baptist Churches (iv, 231 p. mimeo., Sept. 1941)     42-13927

        Society of Friends. (iii, 80 p. mimeo., May 1939)     39-26791 Rev.

TENNESSEE:
    Inventory of the Church and Synagogue Archives of Tennessee:

        Tennessee Baptist Convention:
            Nashville Baptist Association. (iv, 69 p. mimeo., December 1939)     40-26218 Rev.

            Ocoee Baptist Association. (vii, 134 p. mimeo., February 1942)     42-14605

        Jewish Congregations. (iv, 55 p. mimeo., July 1941)     41-23366

        Outline of Development of Methodism in Tennessee. (iv, 16 p. mimeo., December 1940)

UTAH:
    Inventory of the Church Archives of Utah:

        Vol. 1. History and Bibliography of Religion. (iii, 121 p. mimeo., June 1940)     40-28599

        Vol. 2. Baptist Church. (v, 71 p. mimeo., Aug. 1940)

        Vol. 3. Smaller Denominations. (iv, 73 p. mimeo., February 1941)

VERMONT:
    Inventory of the Church Archives of Vermont:

        No. 1. Protestant Episcopal. Diocese of Vermont (iv, 253 p. mimeo., 1940)     40-26758

        Preprint of Churches of Hinesburg, 1789-1939. (iv, 13 p. mimeo., May 1939)

VIRGINIA:
    Inventory of the Church Archives of Virginia:

        Dover Baptist Association. (xxiii, 56 p. mimeo., November 1939)     40-26248 Rev.

        Negro Baptist Churches in Richmond. (xii, 59 p. mimeo., June 1940)     41-12020

## CHURCH ARCHIVES PUBLICATIONS (Cont'd)

**WASHINGTON:**
    Inventory of the Church Archives of Washington:
        Survey of Everett, Yakima, and Wenatchee Church Archives. (20 p. printed in the Pacific Northwest Quarterly, vol. 30, no. 4, pp. 417-436)

        Survey of Seattle Church Archives. (29 p. printed in the Pacific Northwest Quarterly, vol. 28, no. 2, pp. 163-191; also reprint)

        Survey of Spokane Church Archives. (21 p. printed in the Pacific Northwest Quarterly, vol. 28, no. 4, pp. 383-403; also reprint)

**WEST VIRGINIA:**
    Inventory of the Church Archives of West Virginia:
        Presbyterian Churches. (xiv, 301 p. mimeo., December 1941)      42-13926

        Protestant Episcopal Church. (v, 119 p. mimeo., June 1939)      39-26772 Rev.

        Preliminary Bibliography of Material Relating to Churches in West Virginia, Virginia, Kentucky and Southern Ohio. (iv, 15 p. mimeo., December 1940)      40-28945

**WISCONSIN:**
    Inventory of the Church Archives of Wisconsin:
        History of the Southern Wisconsin District of the Evangelical Lutheran Synod of Missouri and other States. (Translation of work by Otto F. Hattstaedt) (ix, 96 p. mimeo., September 1941)      42-13658
        Protestant Episcopal Church:
            Diocese of Eau Claire. (xvi, 135 p. mimeo., 1942)

            Diocese of Fond du Lac. (x, 188 p. mimeo., February 1942)

        Assemblies of God. (v, 73 p. mimeo., April 1942)      42-17652

        Disciples of Christ. (v, 83 p. mimeo., May 1942)      42-17657

        Jewish Congregations. (v, 64 p. mimeo., 1942)

        Moravian Church. (iv, 57 p. mimeo., November 1938)      39-26435 Rev.

        Roman Catholic Church: Diocese of La Crosse. (xiv, 237 p. mimeo., 1942)      42-17649

        United Brethren in Christ. (iv, 136 p. mimeo., April 1940)      41-13958

## CHURCH ARCHIVES PUBLICATIONS (Cont'd)

### Church Directories:

**ARIZONA:**
    Directory of Churches and Religious Organizations in Arizona (iv, 113 p. mimeo., March 1940)

**ARKANSAS:**
    Directory of Churches and Religious Organizations in Arkansas. (ix, 176 p. mimeo., May 1942)     42-24214

**CALIFORNIA, NORTHERN:**
    Directory of Churches and Religious Organizations in Alameda County, California. (iv, 80 p. mimeo., April 1940)     42-14608

    Directory of Churches and Religious Organizations in San Francisco, California. (iv, 118 p. mimeo., May 1941)     42-13708

**CALIFORNIA, SOUTHERN:**
    Directory of Churches and Religious Organizations in Los Angeles County. (vi, 329 p. mimeo., April 1940)     40-26611 Rev.

    Directory of Churches and Religious Organizations in San Diego County. (vi, 96 p. mimeo., June 1940)     42-13706

**DELAWARE:**
    Directory of Churches and Religious Organizations in Delaware (xii, 154 p. mimeo., 1942)     42-19624

**DISTRICT OF COLUMBIA:**
    Directory of Churches and Religious Organizations in the District of Columbia, 1939. (prelim. ed., v, 188 p. mimeo., February 1939)

**FLORIDA:**
    A Preliminary List of Religious Bodies in Florida. (vi, 239 p. mimeo., June 1939)

**IDAHO:**
    Directory of Churches and Religious Organizations of Idaho. (iv, 129 p. mimeo., August 1940)

**ILLINOIS:**
    Directory of Negro Baptist Churches in the U. S.     42-24213
        Vol. 1 (ix, 334 p. mimeo., February 1942)
        Vol. 2. (v, 353 p. mimeo., February 1942)

## CHURCH ARCHIVES PUBLICATIONS (Cont'd)

### Church Directories: (Cont'd)

**INDIANA:**
    Directory of Churches and Religious Organizations in Indiana:
        Vol. I. Marion County. (vii, 119 p. mimeo., July 1940)
        Vol. II. Calument Region (Lake, Porter and LaPorte Counties) (vii, 102 p. mimeo., August 1941)
        Vol. III. Northern Indiana. Pt. I. Adventist Bodies-Mennonite Bodies (vii, 239 p. mimeo., September 1941)
            Pt. II. Methodist - Y.W.C.A. (ii, 240-477 p. mimeo., September 1941)

**IOWA:**
    Directory of Church and Religious Organizations in Iowa

**LOUISIANA:**
    Directory of Churches and Religious Organizations in New Orleans. (iv, 96 p. mimeo., March 1941)      41-14178

**MAINE:**
    Directory of Churches and Religious Organizations in Maine. (iii, 166 p. mimeo., July 1940)

**MICHIGAN**
    Directory of Churches and Religious Organizations in Greater Detroit (x, 164 p. mimeo., December 1941)      42-13929

**MINNESOTA:**
    Directory of Churches and Religious Organizations in Minnesota (xix, 583 p. mimeo., January 1942)      42-19635

**MONTANA:**
    Directory of Churches and Religious Organizations in Montana (iv, 126 p. mimeo., June 1941)      42-13912

**NEW JERSEY:**
    Directory of Churches in New Jersey:      41-52625
        Vol. I. Atlantic County. (44 p. mimeo., Dec. 1940)
        Vol. II. Bergen County. (80 p. mimeo., February 1941)
        Vol. III. Burlington County. (54 p. mimeo., Dec. 1940)
        Vol. IV. Camden County. (72 p. mimeo., December 1940)
        Vol. V. Cape May County. (33 p. mimeo., January 1941)
        Vol. VI. Cumberland County. (42 p. mimeo., Jan. 1941)
        Vol. VIII. Essex County. (121 p. mimeo., March 1941)
        Vol. IX. Hudson County. (90 p. mimeo., April 1941)
        Vol. X. Hunterdon County. (27 p. mimeo., November 1940)
        Vol. XI. Mercer County. (51 p. mimeo., June 1940)
        Vol. XII. Middlesex County. (56 p. mimeo., February 1941)
        Vol. XIII. Monmouth County. (73 p. mimeo., January 1941)
        Vol. XIV. Morris County. (45 p. mimeo., December 1940)
        Vol. XV. Ocean County. (27 p. mimeo., May 1941)

## CHURCH ARCHIVES PUBLICATIONS (Cont'd)

Church Directories: (Cont'd)

NEW JERSEY:
    Directory of Churches in New Jersey: (Cont'd)
        Vol. XVI.   Passaic County. (69 p. mimeo., January 1941)
        Vol. XVII.  Salem County. (22 p. mimeo., November 1940)
        Vol. XVIII. Somerset County. (38 p. mimeo., January 1941)
        Vol. XIX.  Sussex County. (24 p. mimeo., July 1940)
        Vol. XX.   Union County. (71 p. mimeo., January 1941)
        Vol. XXI.  Warren County. (21 p. mimeo., March 1941)

NEW MEXICO:
    Directory of Churches and Religious Organizations in New Mexico. (ix, 385 p. mimeo., July 1940)     40-28671

OKLAHOMA:
    Preliminary List of Churches and Religious Organizations in Oklahoma. Vol. 1. (x, 343 p. mimeo., May 1942)     42-19623

OREGON:
    Directory of Church and Religious Organizations: State of Oregon. (iv, 304 p. mimeo., July 1940)     40-28613

RHODE ISLAND:
    Directory of Churches and Religious Organizations of Rhode Island. (iv, 128 p. mimeo., December 1939)     40-26249

TENNESSEE:
    Directory of Churches, Missions and Religious Institutions of Tennessee.     41-9818

        No. 19. Davidson County. (v, 79 p. mimeo., May 1940)

        No. 33. Hamilton County. (vi, 75 p. mimeo., December 1940)

        No. 47. Knox County (vi, 99 p. mimeo., September 1941)

        No. 79. Shelby County (ix, 114 p. mimeo., May 1941)

        No. 90. Washington County (vi, 47 p. mimeo., January 1942)

UTAH:
    Directory of Churches and Religious Organizations in Utah - except Latter-Day Saints. (iii, 16 p. mimeo., September 1938)

CHURCH ARCHIVES PUBLICATIONS (Cont'd)

Church Directories: (Cont'd)

VERMONT:
    Directory of Churches and Religious Organizations in the State of Vermont. (iv, 122 p. mimeo., August 1939)      39-29380 Rev.

WISCONSIN:
    Directory of Churches and Religious Organizations in Wisconsin. (ix, 358 p. mimeo., January 1941)      41-14177

    Directory of Catholic Churches in Wisconsin. (x, 213 p. mimeo., February 1942)      42-19740

WYOMING:
    Directory of Churches and Religious Organizations in the State of Wyoming. (iii, 64 p. mimeo., July 1939)

## MANUSCRIPT PUBLICATIONS

Guide to Depositories of Manuscript Collections in the United States -- One Hundred Sample Entries. (iii,134 p. mimeo., 1938)     39-26176

"List of Manuscript Accessions in Various Depositories in the United States Received during the Year 1940" in the Annual Report of the American Historical Association for the Year 1941. Vol. I, 191-331 p.

**ARIZONA:**

The Private Journal of George Whitwell Parsons. (vi, 333 p. mimeo., November 1939)

Journal of the Pioneer and Walker Districts, 1863-65. (vii, 158 p. mimeo., August 1941)

**CALIFORNIA, NORTHERN:**

Calendar of the Major Rink Snyder Collection of the Society of California Pioneers. (ii, 107 p. mimeo., June 1940)     40-28471

**CALIFORNIA, SOUTHERN:**

Guide to Depositories of Manuscript Collections in the United States: California. (vii, 75 p. mimeo., October 1941)*     43-2548

Calendar of the Montana Papers in the William Andrews Clark Memorial Library, University of California at Los Angeles. (v, 130 p. mimeo., March 1942)

Calendar of the Francis Bret Harte Letters in the William Andrews Clark Memorial Library, University of California at Los Angeles. (ix, 35 p. mimeo., March 1942)     42-17364

Inventory of the Bixby Collection in the Palos Verdes Library and Art Gallery. (iii, 43 p. mimeo., October 1940)     40-29274

List of the Letters and Manuscripts of Musicians in the William Andrews Clark Memorial Library, University of California at Los Angeles. (iii, 12 p. mimeo., May 1940)     40-28353

List of the Letters and Documents of Rulers and Statesmen in the William Andrews Clark Memorial Library, University of California at Los Angeles. (vii, 16 p. mimeo., January 1941)     41-52714

---

*Includes both Northern and Southern California

## MANUSCRIPT PUBLICATIONS (Cont'd)

DISTRICT OF COLUMBIA:

    Calendar of Alexander Graham Bell Correspondence in the Volta Bureau, Washington, D. C. (v, 41 p. mimeo., April 1940)    40-26489

    Calendar of the Letters and Documents of Peter Force on the Mecklenburg Declaration of Independence in the Loomis Collection, Washington, D. C. (v, 35 p. mimeo., April 1940) 40-26757

    Calendar of the Writings of Frederick Douglass in the Frederick Douglass Memorial Home, Anacostia, D. C., Preliminary Edition. (viii, 93 p. mimeo., December 1940)    41-52933

FLORIDA:

    Guide to Depositories of Manuscript Collections in the United States: Florida. (v, 28 p. mimeo., April 1940)    40-28596

    A List of the Materials in the Austin Carey Memorial Collection in the University of Florida. (xlix, 47 p. mimeo., December 1941)    42-16592

ILLINOIS:

    Guide to Depositories of Manuscript Collections in Illinois. Preliminary Edition. (xi, 55 p. mimeo., June 1940)    40-29366

    Calendar of the Robert Weidensall Correspondence, 1861-1865, at George Williams College, Chicago, Illinois. (xiii, 34 p. mimeo., February 1940)    40-26389

    Calendar of the Ezekiel Cooper Collections of Early American Methodist Manuscripts, 1785-1839. (xi, 97 p. mimeo., January 1941)    41-50037

IOWA:

    Guide to Depositories of Manuscript Collections in the United States: Iowa. (vi, 47 p. mimeo., June 1940)    43-2507

    Guide to Manuscript Collections in Iowa. Vol. I. (v, 57 p. mimeo., September 1940)    42-363

    Diary of E. P. Burton, Surgeon, 7th Regiment, Illinois. (v, 92 p. mimeo., September 1939)    40-26345

## MANUSCRIPT PUBLICATIONS (Cont'd)

LOUISIANA:

"Guide to Depositories of Manuscript Collections in Louisiana"
in The Louisiana Historical Quarterly, Vol. 24, No. 2.
(305-353 p., April 1941) Reprint. (51 p. April 1941)
Second Edition. (iv, 48 p. mimeo., November 1941)   43-2550

Guide to Manuscript Collections in Louisiana: The Department
of Archives, Louisiana State University, Vol. I. (iv, 55 p.
mimeo., August 1940). Second Edition, (vi, 108 p. multi.,
December 1940)   40-28612

Calendar of Manuscript Collections in Louisiana: Series I.
The Department of Archives: No. 1. Taber Collection.
(12 p. printed, May 1938)   38-28419

An Inventory of the Collections of the Middle America Research
Institute:   40-26219 Rev.

    No. 1. Callender I. Fayssoux Collection of William
Walker Papers. (ii, 28 p. mimeo., May 1937)

    No. 2. Calendar of the Yucatecan Letters. (viii, 240 p.
mimeo., October 1939)

    No. 3. Maps in the Frederick L. Hoffman Collection.
(viii, 146 p. mimeo., December 1939)

    No. 4. Maps in the Library of the Middle American Research
Institute. (ix, 282 p. mimeo., November 1941)

"Mississippi River Ice at New Orleans," in The Louisiana
Historical Quarterly, Vol. 21, (349-353 p., 1938)

Transcriptions of Manuscript Collections of Louisiana: No. 1.
The Favrot Papers:   40-28673

    Vol. I.   1695-1769. (iv, 123 p. mimeo., February 1940)

    Vol. II.  1769-1781. (x, 184 p. mimeo., December 1940)

    Vol. III. 1781-1792. (x, 166 p. mimeo., March 1941)

    Vol. IV.  1793-1796. (xiii, 140 p. mimeo., June 1941)

    Vol. V.   1796-1799. (v, 145 p. mimeo., August 1941)

    Vol. VI.  1799-1801. (vii, 141 p. mimeo., October 1941)

    Vol. VII. 1801-1803. (vii, 230 p. mimeo., March 1942)

    Vol. IX.  (1812)    (ii, 108 p. mimeo., February 1941)

## MANUSCRIPT PUBLICATIONS (Cont'd)

**MAINE:**

Index to A Reference List of Manuscripts Relating to the History of Maine, Part III in The Maine Bulletin Vol. XLIII No. 8. (xvi, 211 p. printed, February 1941)

**MARYLAND:**

Calendar of the General Otho Holland Williams Papers in the Maryland Historical Society. (ix, 454 p. mimeo., November 1940)     40-28949

**MASSACHUSETTS:**

Guide to Depositories of Manuscript Collections in Massachusetts. Preliminary Edition. (v, 160 p. mimeo., May 1939)     40-26130

Guide to the Manuscript Collections in the Worcester Historical Society. (iii, 56 p. mimeo., 1941)     42-16158

A Description of the Manuscript Collections in the Massachusetts Diocesan Library. (x, 81 p. mimeo., February 1939)     39-26523

Calendar of the Ryder Collection of Confederate Archives at Tufts College. (v, 165 p. mimeo., 1940)     40-29049

Calendar of the General Henry Knox Papers, Chamberlain Collection, Boston Public Library. (iv, 19 p. mimeo., May 1939)     40-26265

Calender of the Letters of Charles Robert Darwin to Asa Gray. (vii, 148 p. mimeo., December 1939)     40-26267

Diary and Journal (1755-1807) of Seth Metcalf. (iii, 31 p. mimeo., October 1939)     40-26131

**MICHIGAN:**

Guide to Manuscript Depositories in the United States: Michigan. (v, 75 p. mimeo., May 1940)     43-2506

Guide to Manuscript Collections in Michigan:
  Vol. I. Michigan Historical Collections, University of Michigan. (xiv, 239 p. mimeo., September 1941)

  Vol. II. University of Michigan Collections. (ix, 100 p. mimeo., June 1942)

Calendar of the Baptist Collection of Kalamazoo College, Kalamazoo, Michigan. (iv, 194 p. mimeo., December 1940)     41-14070

Calendar of John C. Dancey Correspondence, 1898-1910. (v, 27 p. mimeo., April 1941).     42-1470

MANUSCRIPT PUBLICATIONS (Cont'd)

MINNESOTA:
    Guide to Depositories of Manuscript Collections in the United States:
       Minnesota. (84 p. mimeo., March 1941)     43-2508

MISSOURI:
    Guide to Depositories of Manuscript Collections in the United States:
       Missouri. Preliminary Edition. (iv, 17 p. mimeo., November 1940)
                                                                                                               41-52710

    Information Concerning the Manuscript Depository Collection of the
       Missouri Baptist Historical Society, Liberty, Missouri. (Re-
       printed with additions, from "Guide to Depositories of Manuscript
       Collections in the United States: Missouri,") (iv, 4 p. mimeo.,
       January 1941)     42-1166

MONTANA:
    Bibliography of Graduate Theses in the University of Montana.
       (vii, 71 pages mimeo., January 1942)     42-37230

NEBRASKA:
    Guide to Depositories of Manuscript Collections in the United States:
       Nebraska. Preliminary Edition. (vii, 43 p. mimeo., June 1940)
                                                                                                              42-15369

NEW HAMPSHIRE:
    Guide to Depositories of Manuscript Collections in the United States:
       New Hampshire. (v. 44 p. mimeo., August 1940)     42-15370

NEW JERSEY:
    Guide to Manuscript Depositories in the United States: New Jersey.
       Preliminary edition. (62 p. mimeo., January 1941)     42-3815

    Calendar of the New Jersey State Library Manuscript Collection in
       the Cataloguing Room, State Library, Trenton, New Jersey.
       (iv, 168 p. mimeo., July 1939)     39-29379 Rev.

    Calendar of the Stevens Family Papers, Lieb Memorial Library,
       Stevens Institute of Technology, Hoboken, New Jersey:
       Prelim. Vol. (v, 112 p. mimeo., March 1940)     41-14721

       Vol. I. 1664-1750. (226 p. mimeo., December 1940)

       Vol. II. 1751-1777. (viii, 194 p. mimeo., November 1941)

    Index of the Official Register of the Officers and Men of
    New Jersey in the Revolutionary War. (ix, 124 p. mimeo.,
    April 1941)     42-15485

## MANUSCRIPT PUBLICATIONS (Cont'd)

NEW YORK CITY:
    Guide to Manuscript Depositories in New York City. (150 p. multi., February 1941)      41-20195

NEW YORK STATE:
    Guide to Depositories of Manuscript Collections in New York State. Vol. I. (xxii, 424 p. mimeo., December 1941)

    Guide to Ten Major Depositories of Manuscript Collections in New York State. (vi, 78 p. printed, 1941)

    Calendar of the Gerrit Smith Papers in the Syracuse University Library.      41-52964

        Vol. I, 1819-1846. (ix, 290 p. mimeo., July 1941)

        Vol. II, 1846-1854. (xi, 266 p. mimeo., June 1942)

NORTH CAROLINA:
    Guide to Depositories of Manuscript Collections in the United States: North Carolina. (18 p. printed, July 1940)

    Guide to the Manuscript Collections in the Archives of the North Carolina Historical Commission. (v, 216 p. printed, Feb. 1942)      42-36765

    Guide to the Manuscript Collections in the Duke University Library. (v, 165 p. mimeo., June 1939)      39-29007

    Guide to the Manuscripts in the Archives of the Moravian Church in America, Southern Province, Winston-Salem, North Carolina (vii, 136 p. mimeo., March 1942)      42-24072

    Guide to the Manuscripts in the Southern Historical Collection of the University of North Carolina. (viii, 204 p. printed, 1941)      41-52379

    A Calendar of the Bartlett Yancey Papers in the Southern Historical Collection of the University of North Carolina (iv, 48 p. mimeo., February 1940)      40-26390

    List of the Papeles Procedentes De Cuba (Cuban Papers) in the Archives in the North Carolina Historical Commission (vi, 78 p. mimeo., June 1942)

## MANUSCRIPT PUBLICATIONS (Cont'd)

PENNSYLVANIA:

    Guide to Manuscript Collections in the Historical Society of Pennsylvania. (xiv, 350 p. printed, 1940)     41-8044

    Descriptive Catalogue of the Du Simitiere Papers in the Library Company of Philadelphia. (iv, 196 p. mimeo., April 1940)   40-26649

    The Papers of Colonel Henry Bouquet
- Series 21631) and 21632) (xviii, 170 p. mimeo., 1941)
- Series 21634, (xii, 312 p. mimeo., 1940)
- Series 21643, (xii, 282 p. mimeo., 1941)
- Series 21644, Part I. (ix, 236 p. mimeo., 1941)
  - Part II. (ix, 245 p. mimeo., 1941)
- Series 21645, (xii, 290 p. mimeo., 1941)
- Series 21646, (xii, 259 p. mimeo., 1941)
- Series 21647, (xii, 260 p. mimeo., 1942)
- Series 21648, Part I. (xii, 182 p. mimeo., 1942)
  - Part II. (xii, 200 p. mimeo., 1942)
- Series 21649, Part I. (xii, 262 p. mimeo., 1942)
  - Part II. (1942)
- Series 21650, (1942)
- Series 21652, (lx, 313 p. mimeo., 1940)
- Series 21653, (xiv, 398 p. mimeo., 1940)
- Series 21654, (xv, 285 p. mimeo., 1941)

    Wilderness Chronicles of Northwestern Pennsylvania (xix, 342 p. printed, 1941)

    Calendar of the Joel R. Poinsett Papers in the Henry D. Gilpin Collection. (xv, 264 p. printed, 1941)     41-12586

    Journal of Choussegros de Lery. (ii, 118 p. mimeo., 1940)

    The Expedition of Baron de Longueuil. (16 p. mimeo., 1940)     42-36885
        Revision. (17 p. mimeo., 1941)

    Travels in New-France by J. C. B. (xiv, 167 p. printed 1941)     42-36718

    The Venango Trail. (ii, 52 p. mimeo., 1940)     40-28373

TENNESSEE:

    Guide to Depositories of Manuscript Collections in Tennessee. (iv, 27 p. printed, December 1940)     41-52360

    Guide to Collections of Manuscripts in Tennessee. (vi, 38 p. mimeo., March 1941)     42-3424

## MANUSCRIPT PUBLICATIONS (Cont'd)

**NORTH DAKOTA:**
    Bibliography of Theses Prepared at the University of North Dakota.
        (iv, 62 p. mimeo., December 1940)         40-28929

**OHIO:**
    Calendar of the Joshua Reed Giddings Manuscripts in the Library
        of the Ohio State Archaeological and Historical Society,
        Columbus, Ohio -- Twenty-five Sample Pages. (iv, 29 p. mimeo.,
        December 1939)

    Inventory of Business Records: The D. Connelly Boiler Company;
        The Savage Company. (xiv, 104 p. multi., May 1941)     42-10357

**OREGON:**
    Guides to Depositories of Manuscript Collections in the United
        States: Oregon-Washington. (iv, 42 p. mimeo., December 1940)
                                                            42-15486

    Guides to the Manuscript Collections of the Oregon Historical
        Society. (ii, 133 p. mimeo., August 1940)         40-28670

    The Diary of Basil N. Longsworth, Oregon Pioneer. (iii, 68 p.
        mimeo., November 1938)         39-26344 Rev.

    The Diary of Eli Sheldon Glover, October-December, 1875.
        (vi, 41 p. mimeo., November 1939)         39-28862

    Abstract of Willamette Valley and Cascade Mountain Road Company,
        1864-1911. (42 p. mimeo., 1937)

    Corvallis to Crescent City, California in 1874. (43 p. mimeo.,
        1937)

    Daily Sales of an Auburn Store in 1868. (55 p. mimeo., 1937)

    Letter from Lukiamute Valley in 1846. (4 p. mimeo., 1937)

**PENNSYLVANIA:** *
    Guide to Depositories of Manuscript Collections in Pennsylvania.
        (v, 126 p. printed, September 1939)         39-28788

---

*Frontier Forts and Trails Survey and Historical Records Survey
became Pennsylvania Historical Survey, January 1941.

## MANUSCRIPT PUBLICATIONS (Cont'd)

VERMONT:
    Calendar of the Ira Allen Papers in the Wilbur Library of the University of Vermont. (v, 149 p. mimeo., August 1939)     39-29276 Rev.

WASHINGTON:
    Guides to Depositories of Manuscript Collections in the United States: Oregon-Washington. (iv, 42 p. mimeo., December 1940)     42-15486

WEST VIRGINIA:
    Calendar of the Arthur I. Boreman Letters in the State Department of Archives and History. (iv, 91 p. mimeo., January 1939)     39-26265

    Calendar of the William E. Stevenson Letters in the State Department of Archives and History. (v, 105 p. mimeo., March 1939)     39-26434

    Calendar of the J. J. Jacob Letters in West Virginia Depositories. (vii, 251 p. mimeo., July 1940)     40-28600

    Calendar of the Francis Harrison Pierpont Letters and Papers in West Virginia Depositories. (iv, 387 p. mimeo., October 1940)     40-28681

    Calendar of the Governor Henry Mason Matthews Letters & Papers in the State Department of Archives & History (vi, 327 p. mimeo., October 1941)     42-1615

WISCONSIN:
    Guide to Manuscript Depositories in Wisconsin. (vii, 36 p. mimeo., January 1941)     41-52711

    A Guide to the Manuscript Collections in the Wisconsin Historical Society.

## AMERICAN IMPRINTS INVENTORIES

Location Symbols for Libraries in the United States. (v, 258 p. mimeo., September 1939)     39-29351

Location Symbols for Libraries in the United States. Additions and Corrections, January 1941. (ii, 36 p. mimeo., November 1941)     39-29351

A Hand-List of American Publishers, 1876-1900 (Compiled from the lists of publishers in Frederick Leypoldt's American Catalogue 1876-1900) (ii, 43 p. mimeo., November 1940)

ALABAMA:
    No. 8. Check List of Alabama Imprints, 1807-1840. (ix, 79 p. mimeo., December 1939)     40-26269

ARIZONA:
    No. 3. Check List of Arizona Imprints, 1860-1890. (iii, 41 p. mimeo., July 1938)     39-4907

ARKANSAS:
    No. 39. A Check List of Arkansas Imprints, 1821-1876. (iv, 139 p. mimeo., April 1942)     42-17366

CALIFORNIA:
    No. 31. A Check List of California Non-Documentary Imprints, 1833-1855. (xvii, 109 p., mimeo., April 1942)

IDAHO:
    No. 13. A Check List of Idaho Imprints, 1839-1890. (74 p. mimeo., 1940)     41-50084

ILLINOIS:
    No. 4. Check List of Chicago Ante-Fire Imprints, 1851-1871. (x, 364 p. mimeo., November 1938)     39-4906

    No. 11. A Check List of the Kellogg Collection of "Patent Inside" Newspapers of 1876. (ix, 99 p. mimeo., October 1939)

IOWA:
    No. 15. A Check List of Iowa Imprints, 1838-1860. (84 p. mimeo., December 1940)     42-17567

KANSAS:
    No. 10. Check List of Kansas Imprints, 1854-1876. (xix, 387 p. mimeo., October 1939)     40-3090

KENTUCKY:
    No. 5. Check List of Kentucky Imprints, 1787-1810. (xiv, 205 p. mimeo., 1939)     39-4909

## AMERICAN IMPRINTS INVENTORY (Cont'd)

KENTUCKY: (Cont'd)

    No. 6. Check List of Kentucky Imprints, 1811-1820. (vii, 235 p. mimeo., November 1939)     40-1996

    No. 38. *Supplemental Check List of Kentucky Imprints 1788-1820 (xii, 241 p. mimeo., March 1942)     43-2549

LOUISIANA:

    No. 19. Bibliography of the Official Publications of Louisiana, 1803-1934. (xiv, 579 p. multi., February 1942)     42-19598

MASSACHUSETTS:

    No. 40. A Check List of Massachusetts Imprints, 1801. (xxxii, 157 p. multi., 1942)

    No. 45. A Check List of Massachusetts Imprints, 1802. (xxxiii, 158 p. multi., 1942)     43-444

MICHIGAN:

    No. 52. Preliminary Check List of Michigan Imprints, 1796-1850. (x, 224 p. mimeo., 1942)

MINNESOTA:

    No. 2. Check List of Minnesota Imprints, 1849-1865. (v, 110 p. mimeo., May 1938)     38-22260

MISSOURI:

    No. 1. A Preliminary Check List of Missouri Imprints, 1808-1850. (v, 113 p. mimeo., November 1937)     39-4905

NEBRASKA:

    No. 26. A Check List of Nebraska-Non-Documentary Imprints, 1847-1876. (x, 132 p. mimeo., March 1942)     42-16593

NEVADA:

    No. 7. A Check List of Nevada Imprints, 1859-1890. (xv, 127 p. mimeo., June 1939)     39-29057

NEW JERSEY:

    No. 9. Check List of New Jersey Imprints, 1784-1800. (x, 95 p. mimeo., September 1939)     40-26270

NEW MEXICO:

    No. 25. Check List of New Mexico Imprints and Publications, 1784-1876. (xiii, 115 p. mimeo., February 1942)

NEW YORK STATE:

    No. 12. A Check List of Imprints of Sag Harbor, Long Island, 1791-1820. (xxi, 61 p. mimeo., 1939)     40-26221

    No. 29. A Check List of American Imprints of Batavia, New York. 1819-1876.

---

* Erroneously appeared as No. 25.

## AMERICAN IMPRINTS INVENTORIES (Cont'd)

**NEW YORK STATE:** (Cont'd)

    No. 36. A Check List of Utica N. Y. Imprints, 1799-1830. (viii, 179 p. mimeo., March 1942)

**OHIO:**

    No. 17. A Check List of Ohio Imprints Prior to 1820. (202 p. mimeo., 1941)      42-17565 Rev.

**TENNESSEE:**

    No. 16. Check List of Tennessee Imprints, 1793-1840, in Tennessee Libraries. (viii, 97 p. mimeo., May 1941)      41-52927

    No. 20. Check List of Tennessee Imprints, 1841-1850. (xiii, 138 p. mimeo., December 1941)      42-17566

    No. 32. Check List of Tennessee Imprints, 1793-1840. (xv, 285 p. mimeo., March 1942)

**TEXAS:**

    No. 47. A Check List of Texas Imprints, 1848-1860.

    No. 48. A Check List of Texas Imprints, 1861-1876.

**WASHINGTON:**

    No. 44. A Check List of Washington Imprints, 1853-1876. (89 p. mimeo., April 1942)      42-21716

**WEST VIRGINIA:**

    No. 14. A Check List of West Virginia Imprints, 1791-1830. (62 p. mimeo., December 1940)      41-50571

**WISCONSIN:**

    No. 23. A Check List of Wisconsin Imprints, 1833-1849. (xvi, 176 p. mimeo., 1942)      42-16157 Rev.

    No. 24. A Check List of Wisconsin Imprints, 1850-1854. (xvii, 132 p. mimeo., March 1942)      42-16157 Rev.

    No. 41. A Check List of Wisconsin Imprints, 1855-1858. (xvii, 164 p. mimeo., 1942)      42-16157 Rev.

    No. 42. A Check List of Wisconsin Imprints, 1859-1863. (xvii, 158 p. mimeo., 1942)      42-16157 Rev.

**WYOMING:**

    No. 18. A Check List of Wyoming Imprints, 1866-1890. (69 p. mimeo., 1941)      42-14492

### Imprints Memoranda

**FLORIDA:**

    No. 1. A Preliminary Short-Title Check List of Books, Pamphlets and Broadsides Printed in Florida, 1784-1860. (iii, 15 p. mimeo., November 1937)      38-26760

## AMERICAN IMPRINTS INVENTORIES (Cont'd)

IDAHO:
    No. 2. A Short-Title Check List of Books, Pamphlets and Broadsides Printed in Idaho, 1839-1890. (24 p. mimeo., April 1938)      38-26761

A Bibliography of Books and Pamphlets Printed at Canandaigua, New York, 1799-1850. (Being Vol. 21, No. 4 of Grosvenor Library Bulletin, 62-107 p. printed 1939)[1]      40-32840

NEW MARKET, VIRGINIA, Imprints, 1806-1876 A Check List (x, 36 p. printed August 1942)[2]

## NEWSPAPERS:

ARKANSAS:
    Union List of Arkansas Newspapers, 1819-1942, A Partial Inventory of Arkansas Newspaper files available in offices of publishers, libraries and private collections in Arkansas. (v, 240 p. mimeo., 1942)      42-21717

LOUISIANA:
    Louisiana Newspapers, 1794-1940. A Union List of Louisiana Newspaper Files in Offices of Publishers, Libraries and Private Collections. (viii, 295 p. mimeo., October 1941)      42-1002

MASSACHUSETTS:
    Index to Local News in the Hampshire Gazette, Northampton, Massachusetts, 1786-1937.      40-26137
    Vol. 1. Part 1. Northampton - A to M. (iv, 217 p. mimeo., May 1939)

    Vol. 2. Part 1. Northampton - N to Z. Part 2. Hampshire and Franklin Counties, except Northampton. (ii, 224 p. mimeo., May 1939)

    Vol. 3. Part 3. Personal Section. (ii, 295 p. mimeo., April 1939)

MISSISSIPPI:
    A Preliminary Check List of Mississippi Newspaper Files Available in the Mississippi Department of Archives and History, 1805-1940. (v, 102 p. mimeo., February 1942)

    A Preliminary Union List of Mississippi Newspaper Files Available in County Archives, Offices of Publishers, Libraries and Private Collections in Mississippi, 1805-1940. (vi, 323 p. mimeo., July 1942)

---

1. In cooperation with Douglas C. McMurtrie, Editor
2. In cooperation with Lester J. Cappon and Ira V. Brown, Editors.

## AMERICAN IMPRINTS INVENTORIES (Cont'd)

### NEWSPAPERS

**PENNSYLVANIA:**
    Check List of Philadelphia Newspapers Available in Philadelphia,
        1st Edition, 1936 (vi, 115 p. mimeo., 1936)         37-18921
        2nd Edition, with Supplement. (mimeo., 1937)
    Check List of Pennsylvania Newspapers, Vol. I. Philadelphia County.
        (xvi, 321 p. printed 1942.)
    Manual for Newspaper Transcription. (mimeo., 1941).

**TEXAS:**
    Texas Newspapers, 1813-1939. A Union List of Newspaper Files
        Available in Offices of Publishers, Libraries and a number
        of Private Collections. Vol. 1. (xiii, 293 p. mimeo., 1941)
                41-27316

**UTAH:**
    Check List of Newspapers and Magazines Published in Ogden. (iii,
        5 p. mimeo., May 1938)         40-26238

**VERMONT:**
    Index to the Burlington Free Press in the Billings Library, University of Vermont;         40-26391
        Vol. I.    1848-1852   (iv, 333 p. mimeo., 1940)
        Vol. II.   1853-1855   (v, 298 p. mimeo., August 1940)
        Vol. III. 1856-1858   (iv, 348 p. mimeo., September 1940)
        Vol. IV.  1859-1861   (iv, 298 p. mimeo., November 1940)
        Vol. V.   1862-1863   (iv, 242 p. mimeo., January 1941)
        Vol. VI.  1864-1865   (iv, 290 p. mimeo., April 1941)
        Vol. VII. 1866-1867   (iv, 284 p. mimeo., May 1941)
        Vol. VIII.1868       (v, 246 p. mimeo., June 1941)
        Vol. IX.  1869        (v, 287 p. mimeo., December 1941)
        Vol. X.   1870        (v, 306 p. mimeo., April 1942)

**WISCONSIN:**
    A Guide to Wisconsin Newspapers: Iowa County, 1837-1940.
        (xiii, 142 p. mimeo., 1942)         42-23383

## AMERICAN PORTRAIT INVENTORY

Early American Portrait Artists, 1663-1860. (Revision of 1440 Early
American Portrait Artists.) (see New Jersey)*

CONNECTICUT:
    Preliminary Check List of American Portraits, 1620-1825,
        Found in Connecticut. (37 p. mimeo., 1939)

MAINE:
    American Portrait Inventory: American Portraits Found in the
        State of Maine, 1745-1850. Preliminary volume. (iii,
        88 p. multi., 1941)

MASSACHUSETTS:
    American Portraits, 1620-1825, Found in Massachusetts:
        Vol. 1. (vii, 254 p. mimeo., May 1939)

        Vol. 2. (ii, 255-573 p. mimeo., May 1939)

        Known Early American Portrait Painters before 1860
        (13 p. multi., ca 1940)

NEW HAMPSHIRE:
    Preliminary Check List of American Portraits, 1620-1860,
        Found in New Hampshire. (30 p. mimeo., 1942)

NEW JERSEY:
    American Portrait Inventory: 1440 Early American Portrait
        Artists (1663-1860). Preliminary volume. (xii, 305 p.
        mimeo., December 1940)

RHODE ISLAND:
    Preliminary Check List of American Portraits, 1620-1825,
        Found in Rhode Island. (17 p. mimeo., 1939)

---

*Cooperative effort of the Historical Record Survey Projects and
the New York City Art Project.

## GUIDES TO CIVILIAN ORGANIZATIONS

ARIZONA:
    Directory of Community Service Organizations in Arizona.           43-1154
        (ix, 254 p. mimeo., May 1942)

CALIFORNIA:

COLORADO:
    Directory of Community Service Organizations in Colorado.
        (394 p. mimeo., December 1941)

GEORGIA:
    Directory of Community Service Organizations in Georgia:          42-21370
        Vol. I. Southwestern Georgia. (vi, 170 p. mimeo.,
            December 1941)

        Vol. II. Coastal Georgia. (vi, 140 p. mimeo.,
            February 1942)

        Vol. III. Central Georgia. (vi, 178 p. mimeo.,
            January 1942)

        Vol. IV. Northeastern Georgia. (vi, 157 p. mimeo.,
            March 1942)

        Vol. V. Northwestern Georgia. (vi, 136 p. mimeo.,
            April 1942)

KENTUCKY:
    Guide to Civilian Organizations in Kentucky:                      42-18804 Rev
        Allen County. (ii, 12. mimeo., December 1942)
        Ballard County. (i, 14 p. mimeo., June 1942)
        Barren County.
        Bath County.
        Bell County. (ii, 22 p. mimeo., January 1943)
        Bourbon County.
        Boyd County. (ii, 22 p. mimeo., July 1942)
        Breckinridge County. (ii, 18 p. mimeo., December 1942)
        Bullitt County. (ii, 10 p. mimeo., August 1942)
        Caldwell County.
        Callaway County. (ii, 23 p. mimeo., June 1942)
        Campbell County. (iv, 109 p. mimeo., May 1942)
        Carlisle County. (ii, 13 p. mimeo., June 1942)
        Carroll County.
        Casey County. (ii, 13 p. mimeo., January 1943)
        Christian County. (ii, 25 p. mimeo., July 1942)

## GUIDES TO CIVILIAN ORGANIZATIONS (Cont'd)

KENTUCKY: (Cont'd)
    Crittenden County.
    Davies County. (ii, 29 p. mimeo., August 1942)
    Edmondson County. (ii, 10 p. September 1942)
    Fayette County. (iii, 59 p. mimeo., January 1943)
    Fleming County. (ii, 11 p. mimeo., January 1943)
    Fulton County. (ii, 19 p. mimeo., May 1942)
    Gallatin County.
    Garrard County.
    Graves County. (ii, 20 p. mimeo., June 1942)
    Grayson County.
    Hardin County. (ii, 21 p. mimeo., June 1942)
    Harlan County.
    Harrison County.
    Henderson County. (ii, 30 p. mimeo., August 1942)
    Hickman County. (ii, 12 p. mimeo., June 1942)
    Hopkins County.
    Jefferson County. (see Louisville and Jefferson)
    Johnson County.
    Kenton County. (v, 64 p. mimeo., June 1942)
    LaRue County. (11, 11 p. mimeo., July 1942)
    Lawrence County.
    Lee County.
    Logan County. (ii, 27 p. mimeo., October 1942)
    Louisville and Jefferson Counties. (v, 233 p. mimeo., October 1942)
    Lyon County.
    Madison County.
    Marshall County. (ii, 17 p. mimeo., June 1942)
    Mason County.
    McCracken County. (see Paducah and McCracken)
    McLean County. (15 p. mimeo., October 1942).
    Montgomery County. (ii, 17 p. mimeo., January 1943)
    Muhlenberg County. (ii, 23 p. mimeo., August 1942)
    Nelson County.
    Ohio County. (ii, 24 p. mimeo., January 1943)
    Oldham County. (ii, 14 p. mimeo., June 1942)
    Owen County.
    Paducah and McCracken Counties. (iv, 61 p. mimeo., April 1942)
    Pike County. (ii, 22 p. mimeo., August 1942)
    Shelby County. (ii, 18 p. mimeo., September 1942)
    Simpson County.
    Spencer County. (ii, 16 p. mimeo., June 1942)
    Todd County. (ii, 10 p. mimeo., August 1942)
    Trigg County. (ii, 14 p. mimeo., January 1943)
    Union County. (ii, 27 p. mimeo., July 1942)
    Warren County.
    Washington County. (ii, 11 p. mimeo., January 1943)
    Webster County. (ii, 22 p. mimeo., December 1942)

## GUIDES TO CIVILIAN ORGANIZATIONS (Cont'd)

**MONTANA:**
Directory of Community Service Organizations in Montana:
(iii, 231 p., mimeo., March 1942)

**TENNESSEE:**
Inventory of Civilian Organizations Participating in the Nashville Defense Program. (59 p. mimeo., 1942)

**UTAH:**
Directory of Community Service Organizations in Utah.
(iv, 122 p. mimeo., November 1941)

## MISCELLANEOUS PUBLICATIONS

Memorandum on the Annotated Bibliography of
    United States History (ii, 32 p. mimeo., 1937)

Annotated Bibliography of American History
    (Sample entries) (x, 201 p. mimeo., October 1942)

**ARIZONA:**
    The District Courts of the Territory of Arizona, 1864-1912.
        (vii, 38 p. mimeo., May 1941)           41-52934

**CALIFORNIA:**
    Handbook of Sources of Economic Data Pertaining to California
        (Index and List of Publications) 206 p. 1941)     41-8271

**DISTRICT OF COLUMBIA:**
    Bio-bibliographical Index of Musicians in the United States
        of America from Colonial Times. (xxiii, 439 p. mimeo.,
        June 1941)           41-13993

    Commissioner Charles Mason and Clara Barton. In Journal of
        the Patent Office Society, Vol XXII, No. 11. (pp. 802-
        827, November 1940)

**FLORIDA:**
    Check List of Records Required of County Officials Duly
        appointed or Elected According to Constitutional or
        statutory Provisions. (iv, 103 p. mimeo., December 1937)

    Check List of Records Required by Law in Florida Counties.
        (Revised). (v, 89 p. mimeo., August 1939)     39-29277

    Spanish Land Grants in Florida:           40-28679
        Vol. I. Unconfirmed Claims. (lxi, 374 p. mimeo.,
            August 1940)

        Vol. II. Confirmed Claims. A-C. (lix, 371 p. mimeo.,
            November 1940)

        Vol. III. Confirmed Claims. D-J. (lxiii, 341 p. mimeo.,
            March 1941)

        Vol. IV. Confirmed Claims. K-R. (lxiii, 277 p. mimeo.,
            March 1941)

        Vol. V. Confirmed Claims. S-Z. (lxiii, 338 p. mimeo.,
            May 1941)

**GEORGIA:**
    Classified Inventory of Georgia Maps. (xii, 149 p. multi.,
        April 1941)           41-46065
    Notes on F.B.I. School for Police (v, 48 p. mimeo.,
        March 1942)

## MISCELLANEOUS PUBLICATIONS (Cont'd)

INDIANA:
    Check List of Indiana County Records with Introduction on County Governmental Organization. (iii, 128 p. 1937)    42-13049

    State Legislation Pertaining to Archives and Public Records-- Sample Pages for Indiana. (iii, 85 p. mimeo., April 1938)

IOWA:
    Statutory Rights of Women in the United States. (iii, 94 p. mimeo., January 1940)

KENTUCKY:
    Duties and Functions of Kentucky County Government. (ii, 59 p. mimeo., February 1938)

    Guide and Check List of County Governmental Organization and County Record System, Past and Present of Kentucky Counties. (iii, 77 p. mimeo., March 1937)

LOUISIANA:
    County - Parish Boundaries in Louisiana. (vi, 139 p. mimeo., October 1939)    39-29350

    Inventory of the Records of World War Emergency Activities in Louisiana, 1916-1920. (ii, 61 p. mimeo., January 1942)    42-18650

    Judicial and Congressional District Boundary Law in Louisiana. (ii, 90 p. multi., October 1939)    39-29349

MASSACHUSETTS:
    Abstract and Index of the Records of the Inferior Court of Pleas (Suffolk County Court), Held in Boston, 1680-1698. (iii, 224 p. mimeo., 1940)    42-18962

    Index to Proclamations of Massachusetts Issued by Governors and other Authorities:    38-26714
        Vol. 1. 1620-1775. (xiv, 200 p. mimeo., April 1937)

        Vol. 2. 1776-1936. (i, 201-354 p. mimeo., April 1937)

MICHIGAN:
    "In-Migrant Applications for Michigan Automobile Licenses," in <u>Hearings before the Select Committee Investigating National Defense Migration</u>, 77th Cong., 1st. sess., Part 18 <u>Detroit Hearings</u>, Industrial Section, pp. 7587-7603.

    Survey of Automobile Graveyards in Michigan.

    Survey of Auxiliary Shop Training Facilities.

## MISCELLANEOUS PUBLICATIONS (Cont'd)

**MINNESOTA:**

General Legislation Concerning Counties in Minnesota. (iii, 31 p. mimeo., June 1937)

Guide to Historic Markers -- Erected by the State Highway Department Cooperating with the Minnesota Historical Society. (iv, 39 p. mimeo., May 1940)     40-28611

Inventory of Records of World War (I) Emergency Activities. vii, 85 p. mimeo., December 1941)     42-9245

Minnesota Judicial Districts. (vi, 86 p. mimeo., January 1942)     42-14286

Report of the Chippawa Mission Archaeological Investigation. (vi, 42 p. mimeo., February 1941)     41-13411

The Cuyuna Range -- A History of a Minnesota Iron Mining District. (iv, 168 p. mimeo., December 1940)     40-28946

**MISSISSIPPI:**

Sargent's Code -- A Collection of the Original Laws of the Mississippi Territory Enacted 1799-1800 by Governor Winthrop Sargent and the Territorial Judges. (ix, 168 p. mimeo., June 1939)     39-29181

State and County Boundaries of Mississippi. Prelim. edition. (xxii, 150 p. mimeo., July 1942)

**MISSOURI:**

Early History of Missouri. (iii, 18 p. mimeo., August 1941)

Early Missouri Archives:     42-1466
    Vol. I. (viii, 98 p. mimeo., November 1941)
    Vol. II. (iv, 70 p. mimeo., January 1942)
    Vol. III. (11 p. mimeo., March 1942)

County Court Records: St. Charles County. (40 p. mimeo., 1941)

The Organization of Missouri Counties. (19 p. mimeo., 1941)

**MONTANA:**

Abstract of Montana State Laws Relating to the Office of Clerk and Recorder. (41 p. mimeo., 1941)

Abstract of Montana State Laws Relating to the Office of County Treasurer. (59 p. mimeo., December 1940)

Abstract of Montana State Laws Relating to the Office of County Commissioner. (55 p. printed 1942)

## MISCELLANEOUS PUBLICATIONS (Cont'd)

NEW JERSEY:

List and Index of Presidential Executive Orders: Unnumbered Series.

Analysis of Yea-Nay Votes. (xii, 76 p. mimeo., 1941)    42-14287

The Atlas of Congressional Roll Calls, An Analysis of yea-and-nay votes (a prospectus from Columbia University Press). (8 p. printed 1941)

Manual of New Jersey Recording Acts.
Series I. County Requirements, Prelim, edition.
(xvi, 290 p. mimeo., November 1940)    41-52712

NEW MEXICO:

Index to Final Report of Investigations Among the Indians of the Southwestern United States -- Carried on Mainly in the Years 1880-1885 by A. F. Bandelier. (v, 86 p. mimeo., June 1942)

NEW YORK:

List and Index of the Presidential Executive Orders: 1862-1938 - Numbered Series 1-8030, 2 Vols. (1600 p. printed, 1942)

Inventory of Maps (Partial) Located in Various States, County, Municipal and other Public Offices in New York State, exclusive of New York City. (vi, 355 p., mimeo., 1942)

NORTH DAKOTA:

Abstract and Check List of Statutory Requirements for County Records. (vi, 151 p. mimeo., January 1939)    40-33758

1940 Supplement to 1936 North Dakota Municipal Officials Hand Book. (xi, 62 p. mimeo., August 1940)

OHIO:

Historic Sites of Cleveland: Hotels and Taverns. (xxii, 739 p. multi., August 1942)

OKLAHOMA:

Check List of Various Records Required or Permitted by Law in Oklahoma. (67 p. mimeo., January 1937)    37-28805

OREGON:

A Condensed Calendar of Legal Publication Laws (81 p. printed 1942)

Description of County Offices in Oregon and Check List of their Records. (i, 36 p. mimeo., July 1937)    42-2561

Guide to the Angelus Studio Collection of Historical Photographs. (v, 77 p. mimeo., April 1940)    40-28356

MISCELLANEOUS PUBLICATIONS (Cont'd)

OREGON: (Cont'd)
    Inventory of the Records of the Federal Theatre Project
        Records of Oregon. (    p. November 1939)

    Record of Married Women's Separate Property in
        Baker County, 1862-72. ( 5 p. mimeo., 1937)

    Transportation Items from the Weekly Oregonian 1852-1862.
        (13 p. mimeo., 1937)

PENNSYLVANIA:
    Check List of Maps Pertaining to Pennsylvania up to 1900.
        (    p. mimeo., 1935)

        Reprint with Supplement to Check List of Maps to
        Pennsylvania up to 1900. (    p. mimeo., 1936)

    A Description and Analysis of the Bibliography of American
        Literature. (vi, 25 p. printed, January 1941)

    A Partial Bibliography of the Archaeology of Pennsylvania
        and Adjacent States. (45 p. mimeo., 1941)        41-46207

TENNESSEE:
    Check List of Records Required or Permitted by Law in
        Tennessee. (v, 51 p. mimeo., August 1937)

    Instructions for Using County Records as Source Material.
        (i, 16 p. mimeo., January 1939)

    Special Publications Series:        39-29352
        No. 1. Directory of Libraries in Tennessee. (iii,
            17 p. mimeo., August 1939)

        No. 2. History and Organization of the Shelby County
            Judiciary. (iii, 14 p. mimeo., November 1939)

        No. 3. A Summary of General Highway Legislation in
            Tennessee During the Period 1881-1909. (iii, 14 p.
            mimeo., January 1940).

        No. 4. A Summary of Special Legislation Relating to
            The Government of Sullivan County. (ii, 19 p. mimeo.,
            March 1940)

        No. 5. Check List of Acts and Codes of the State of
            Tennessee, 1792-1939. (ii, 21 p. mimeo., June 1940)

## MISCELLANEOUS PUBLICATIONS (Cont'd)

**TEXAS:**
    Check List of Records Required or Permitted by Law in Texas.
        (1v, 86 p. mimeo., January 1937)         37-26429

**UTAH:**
    County Government of the Provisional State of Deseret
        (ii, 9 p. mimeo., August 1937)         42-19875

    Records Required of County Officers, State of Deseret, March 15,
        1849 to April 5, 1851. (3 p. mimeo., August 1937)

**VERMONT:**
    Public Laws of Vermont Relating to Duties of Town Clerks.
        (As amended 1935, 1937, 1939, 1940). (xii, 138 (10) p.
        mimeo., October 1940)         40-28999

**WEST VIRGINIA:**
    West Virginia County Formations and Boundary Changes.
        (iii, 249 p. mimeo., December 1938)         39-26066

    Second edition. (May 1939)

    Cemetery Readings in West Virginia:
        Gideon Magisterial District of Cabell County. (iv,
            320 p. mimeo., February 1940)         39-29192

        Fairmont and Grant Magisterial Districts of Marion
            County. (v, 244 p. mimeo., March 1941)

        Lincoln and Paw Paw Magisterial Districts of Marion
            County. (iv, 207 p. mimeo., September 1939)

    Calendar of Wills:         41-23131
        Upshur County. (viii, 91 p. mimeo., August 1941)

**WISCONSIN:**
    Abstract and Check List of Statutory Requirements for
        County Records. (v, 77 p. mimeo., February 1937)

    Supplement No. 1 to Abstract and Check List. (ii, 8 p.
        mimeo., May 1937)

    An Index to Governors' Messages. (ii, 186 p. mimeo.,
        February 1941)         41-52908

    A Brief History of Galesville University, 1854-1940
        (iii, 106 p. mimeo., 1940)

## MISCELLANEOUS PUBLICATIONS (Cont'd)

WISCONSIN: (Cont'd)

    Development of Town Boundaries in Wisconsin:     41-11457
        No. 9. Chippewa County. (vii, 157 p. mimeo., 1942)

        No. 13. Dane County. (38 p. mimeo., 1942)

        No. 36. Manitowoc County. (iv, 42 p. mimeo., 1941)

        No. 49. Portage County. (vii, 41 p. mimeo., 1942)

    Origin and Legislative History of County Boundaries in
        Wisconsin. (vii, 249 p. mimeo., 1942)     42-20627

APPENDIX I

## MICROFILM

**INDIANA:**

    Allen County:

        Roll 61.    Deed Records (A, B, C, & D) 1824-1842;
Commissioners Records (A, B, & C) 1824-1850.

        Roll 62.    Will Records 1831-1855
Probate Order Book (A & B) 1825-1844.
Civil Order Books (A & B) 1824-1839.
Marriage Records (2 vols.) 1847-1856.

        Roll 63.    Marriage Records (5 vols.) 1857-1872.

        Roll 64.    Marriage Records (5 vols.) 1872-1880.

    Clark County:

        Roll 17.    Probate Order Book (Vol. A) 1817-1828.
Probate Order Book (Vol. B) 1828-1835.
Birth Record 1882-1893, 1899-1907, 1882-1886, 1886-1890, 1888-1891, 1897-1899, 1900-1901, 1901-1907.
Estray Book 1802-1818.
Court Common Pleas 1801-1805, 1806-1808, 1808-1810.

        Roll 18.    Order Book Court Common Pleas 1810-1817.
Court Record 1802-1813.
Minute Book Court Common Pleas 1801-1805, 1801-1803, 1803-1808, 1808-1814.
Minute Book Circuit Court & Commissioners Record 1815-1820.
Commissioners Record 1820-1824, 1824-1828, 1832-1839.

        Roll 19.    Commissioners Record 1839-1843, 1843-1845, 1845-1852.
Seminary Record 1830-1851.
Alien Record (Aliens to become citizens of United States) 1845-1852.
Probate Order Book "C" (Estate of Jonathan Jennings) 1836.
Appraisal and Estates of Jonathan Jennings deceased 1833-1840.

        Roll 58.    Minutes Board Commissioners apportioning lands to Illinois Regiment 1785-1820.
Order Book Court Quarter Sessions (2 vols.) 1801-1808.
Court Order Book (1807-1813).

## MICROFILM (Cont'd)

## INDIANA (Cont'd)

Dearborn County:
- Roll 54. Marriage Records (Book 8 to 13) 1846-1879.
- Roll 54a. Marriage Records (2 vols.) 1880-1889.
- Roll 55. Commissioners Records (5 Books) 1826-1851.
  Surveyors Book 1799-1805.
  Deed Record (Book AA) Prior to 1826.
- Roll 56. Deed Records ("BB" & "CC") Prior to 1826,
  (A to D) 1826-1830.
  Will Record 1824-1832.
  Probate Court Records 1826-1830.
  Order Book Circuit Court (2 vols.) 1824-1829.
- Roll 57. Birth Records (7 vols.) 1882-1907.

Floyd County:
- Roll 13. Marriage Record 1819-1837, 1837-1845,
  1845-1853, 1853-1857, 1858-1864, 1864-1871.
- Roll 14. Marriage Record 1871-1878, 1878-1885, 1885-1891.
  Birth Record 1882-1885, 1885-1887, 1887-1889, 1889-1891.
- Roll 15. Birth Record 1891-1894, 1894-1902, 1897-1903,
  1904-1906, 1903-1907, 1900-1907, 1904-1907.
  Deed Record (Vol. A) 1818-1820, (Vol. B)
  1820-1825. (Vol. C) 1825-1829.
  Will and Probate Record (A) 1818-1829.
- Roll 16. Marriage Record General Index #1 1808-1878,
  #2 1879-1897.
  Marriage Record (Vol. A) 1808-1820, (Vol. B)
  1820-1828, (Vol. C) 1828-1834, (Vol. D.)
  1834-1841.
  Will Record (Vol. A) 1801-1817, (Vol. B) 1817-1833.

Franklin County:
- Roll 48. Issue Docket 1811.
  Court Common Pleas (Minutes of Books "B" and
  "C") 1811-1814.
  Apprentice Record 1831-1853.
  Court Common Pleas 1814.
  Will Records (2 vols.) 1814-1831.
  Probate Order Book 1827-1834.
  Probate Record 1811-1829.
  Order Book Circuit Court (2 vols.) 1815-1819,
  (2 vols.) 1823-1828.

## MICROFILM (Cont'd)

### INDIANA (Cont'd)

**Franklin County:**

Roll 49. Order Book Circuit Court (4 vols.) 1819-1825, (3 vols.) 1828-1836.
Minute Book Circuit Court 1815.
Inventories Estates 1811-1820.
Fee Book Circuit Court 1811-1816.

Roll 50. Marriage Records (2 vols. Index) 1811-1824, (8 vols.) 1811-1868.

Roll 51. Marriage Records (4 vols.) 1868-1890.
Birth Records (4 vols.) 1882-1907.
Brookville Birth Record 1894-1907.
Stock Brands 1811-1839.
Estray Book 1811-1814.
Minute Book Circuit Court 1815-1816.
Reference Docket Circuit Court 1813-1816.
Execution Docket Circuit Court 1811-1816.

Roll 52. Deed Records (7 vols.) 1810-1830.

Roll 53. Marriage Records (Books 1 to 7) 1826-1846.

**Gibson County:**

Roll 34. Will Record (3 vol.) 1813-1834.
Probate Order Book (A) 1817-1830.
Order Book Court Common Pleas and Circuit Court (A) 1813-1818.
Order Book Circuit Court (B) 1820-1821, (C) 1821-1828, 1828-1839.
Common Pleas and Circuit Court 1813-1820.
Commissioners Record 1835-1845.

Roll 35. Commissioners Record 1845-1854.
Birth Records (11 vol.) 1882-1907.

Roll 36. Princeton Birth Records 1882-1907.
Deed Records (Vols. A, B, C, D) 1813-1833.
County Tax List 1819-1826.

Roll 37. Marriage Licenses (3 vol.) 1813-1868.
Marriage Records (3 to 7) 1863-1890.

**Harrison County:**

Roll 7. Estray Book 1809-1817.
Tract Book 1807-1821.
Deed Records (Vol. A) 1809-1817, (Vol. B) 1817-1818, (Vol. C) 1818-1822, (Vol. D) 1822-1826, (Vol. E) 1825-1829.

## MICROFILM (Cont'd)

### INDIANA (Cont'd)

Harrison County:
- Roll 8. Birth Record (A) 1882-1886, (B) 1886-1888, (C) 1888-1890, (D) 1891-1893, (E) 1893-1897, (F) 1897-1900, (G) 1900-1904, (H) 1906-1907.
Manuscript of William Mitchell 1725.
Commissioners Record (A) 1817-1824, (B) (Letters of Corydon Branch Bank) 1825-1830, (C) 1831-1838, (D) 1838-1844.

- Roll 9. Commissioners Record (Vol. E) 1844-1849, (Vol. F) 1849-1853.
Will Record Book (A) 1809-1832.
Seminary Records (in possession of the Griffith Family, Corydon) 1827-1851.
Court Record (partly Probate) 1815-1817.
Probate Court Record 1817-1829.
Court Record 1809-1816, 1814-1817.
Circuit Court Order Book (B) 1820-1825 (C) 1817-1820.

- Roll 10. Court Record 1817-1819.
McClure Workingmens Institute 1855-1858.
Account Book of J. B. Slaughter 1818-1830.
Minute Book Court Common Pleas 1811-1814.
Indices to Marriages 1809-1817 & part 1842-1846.
Marriages 1809-1817, 1817-1832.
Marriage Record (Vol. B) 1826-1852, (Vol. C) 1853-1859. (Vol. E) 1859-1866.

- Roll 11. Marriage Affidavits Vol. 1 1866-1875.
Marriage Record (Vol. F) 1866-1871, (Vol. G) 1872-1875, (Vol. H) 1876-1879, (Vol. I) 1879-1882.

- Roll 12. Marriage Record (Vol. J) 1882-1885, (Vol. K) 1885-1888, (Vol. L) 1888-1892.

Jefferson County:
- Roll 20. Will Record (Vol. A) 1811-1822, (Vol. B) 1822-1827, (Vol. C) 1827-1832.
Civil Order Book 1812-1818.
Circuit Court Record 1811-1819.
Treasurers Book 1812.
License Record (by Treasurer) 1816-1837.
Commissioners Record 1817-1822, 1822-1832, 1836-1838.

MICROFILM (Cont'd)

INDIANA (Cont'd)
    Jefferson County:
        Roll 21.    Commissioners Record 1832-1835, 1838-1840, 1840-1843, 1843-1847, 1847-1850, 1850-1854.
                  Tax List 1827.

        Roll 22.    Birth Record 1882-1896, 1897-1905, 1905-1907, 1882-1890, 1890-1896, 1893-1896, 1896-1900, 1901-1904, 1906-1907.
                  Deed Record Index for Vol. "A" to "F" (inclusive) 1811-1830.
                  Deed Record (Vol. A) 1811-1817, (Vol. B) 1816-1820.

        Roll 23.    Deed Record (Vol. C) 1820-1823, (Vol. D) 1823-1827, (Vol. E) 1827-1829, (Vol. F) 1829-1830.
                  Marriage Record 1811-1832, 1831-1836, 1836-1839.

        Roll 24.    Marriage Record 1839-1841, 1841-1845, 1845-1850, 1850-1853.
                  Marriage Record Indices to Men (9 Vols.) 1853-1891.

    Jennings County:
        Roll 25.    Birth Record 1882-1884, 1885-1888, 1888-1893, 1893-1898 & 1903-1904, 1899-1902, 1904-1907.
                  Circuit Court 1817-1822.
                  Will and Probate Record 1818-1829.
                  Probate Record 1830-1836.
                  Deed Record (Vol. A) 1817-1828, (Vol. B) 1828-1833.

        Roll 26.    Commissioners Record 1824-1836, 1836-1846.
                  Index to Marriage Records 1818-1845.
                  Marriage Record 1818-1830, 1830-1837, 1837-1845, 1845-1850.

        Roll 27.    Marriage Record 1850-1858, 1858-1866, 1866-1873, 1873-1879, 1879-1887.
                  Marriage Returns 1881-1888.

## MICROFILM (Cont'd)

INDIANA (Cont'd)
  Knox County:

  Roll 28.  Register of Negro Slaves 1805-1807.
  Minutes of Orphans Court 1796-1805.
  Minutes of the Court of General Quarter
  Sessions 1796-1801, 1801-1805.
  Chancery Appearance 1806-1810.
  Minutes Court of Chancery 1807-1811.
  Court Common Pleas 1790-1792.
  Minutes Court Common Pleas 1796-1801
  1796-1799, 1801-1806, 1806-1810, 1807-1810,
  1810-1813.
  Circuit Court of Oyer and Terminer,
  General Jail Delivery, and Nisi Prius held
  by Federal Judge 1795,
  Minutes to Circuit Court 1816-1818.
  Order Book Common Pleas 1811-1813 and
  Order Book Circuit Court (A) 1814-1817,
  (B) 1817-1820.

  Roll 29.  Order Book Circuit Court (Vol. C) 1821-1825,
  (Vol. D) 1825-1831.
  Will Record 1806-1852.
  Probate Court Record 1790-1805, 1817-1829
  1829-1832, 1832-1839.
  Poor Relief Record 1821-1832.
  General Index to Deeds 1814-1829.

  Roll 30.  Deed Record (Vol. A) 1814-1817, (B) 1817-
  1822, (C) 1822-1826, (D) 1826-1829.
  Court of Claim 1814-1816 and
  Commissioners Record 1817-1820.
  Commissioners Record (Vol. A) 1823-1839,
  (B) 1839-1847.

  Roll 31.  Commissioners Record (Vol. A) 1827-1855.
  Birth Record 1882-1886, 1886-1898, 1897-1899,
  1899-1901, 1900-1902, 1902-1903, 1903-1904.

  Roll 32.  Birth Record 1904-1905, 1905-1906, 1906-1907,
  Minutes Board Trustees Vincennes University
  1806-1836.
  Birth Record (Vincennes) 1893-1903, 1903-1906.
  Marriage Record (Vol. 4) 1838-1854, (Vol. E)
  1854-1860, (Vol. F) 1860-1866.

  Roll 33.  Marriage Records (G 8, 9, 10) 1866-1883.
  Marriage Returns 1881-1889.
  Estate Judge William Clarke 1802.
  Estate Moses Henry 1790
  George Rogers Clark 1796
  Jonathan Jennings 1807.

## MICROFILM (Cont'd)

## INDIANA (Cont'd)

Knox County, Borough of Vincennes:
- Roll 65. Trustees Proceedings 1815-1816
  Ordinances 1816-1836
  Treasurers Accounts 1819-1840
  Common Records 1818-1837
  Journal of Borough Trustees 1820-1836
  Miscellaneous Papers (Vincennes) 1784-1815c

Perry County:
- Roll 59. Deed Record 1815-1835
  Circuit Court (Complete Record) 1817-1834
  Commissioners Record 1847-1851
  Will Record 1813-1843
  Circuit Court Order Book (2 vols.) 1815-1832
  Marriage Records (2 vols.) 1815-1861.

- Roll 60. Marriage Records (4 vols.) 1861-1890
  Birth Records (3 vols.) 1889-1905.

Posey County:
- Roll 38. Deed Records (Vols. A to E) 1812-1832
  Will Record Index (A), (B) 1816-1852
  Record Circuit Court and Probate Order Book 1815-1827.

- Roll 39. Probate Order 1828-1834
  Circuit Court Order Book (A, B, C) 1815-1829.
  General Index Commissioners Record to Volumes A, B, C, D, E, F, G, H, I, J, K, L, 1817-1855.
  Commissioners Records (A, B, C, D, E, F) 1817-1842.

- Roll 40. Commissioners Records (G, H, I, J, K, L) 1842-1855.
  Birth Records (4 vols.) 1882-1900 a. Vol. 1887-1893 contains records of county Mt. Vernon and New Harmony.

- Roll 41. Birth Records (2 vols.) 1900-1907
  Marriage Record Index Vols. 1 & 2 1815-1846
  Marriage Records (Vols. 1-5) 1815-1868.

- Roll 42. Marriage Records (Vols. 6-8) 1868-1882
  Marriage Returns 1882-1887, 1887-1900.

Scott County:
- Roll 1. Deed Record (A) 1819-1827, (B) 1826-1828
  Land Entry Book
  Commissioners Record (A) 1820-1840, (B) 1841-1851, Vol. 1 1851-1865.

## MICROFILM (Cont'd)

### INDIANA (Cont'd)

Scott County:
- Roll 2. Birth Record Vol. 1 1882-1892, Vol. 2 1888-1895, Vol. 3 1895-1902, Vol. 4 1899-1906, Vol. 5 1902-1907
  Probate Order Book #1 1820-1840, #2 1836-1840
  Marriage Record Vol. 1 1820-1840, Vol. 2 1740-1848, Vol. 3 1848-1861, Vol. 4 1861-1877, Vol. 5 1877-1883, Vol. 6 1883-1897.

Spencer County:
- Last of Roll 46.
  Marriage Records (Vols. 1-6) 1818-1874.

- Roll 47. Marriage Records (Vols. 7 & 8) 1874-1884
  Marriage Returns 1882-1890
  Will and Probate Record 1818-1830
  Deed Records (Vols. A & B) 1818-1835.

Warrick County:
- Roll 43. Deed Records (3 vols.) 1813-1834
  Probate Order Book 1817-1831
  Court of Nisi Prius 1813
  Order Book Court Pleas and Circuit Court 1813-1819.
  Order Book Circuit Court 1818-1838
  Commissioners Record (Index) 1813-1844
  Commissioners Record (2 vols.) 1824-1844

- Roll 44. Commissioners Record 1844-1852
  Marriage Records (Vols. 1-4) 1813-1873.

- Roll 45. Marriage Records (Vols. 5 & 6) 1873-1884
  Marriage Returns 1882-1891
  Birth Records (7 vols.) 1882-1902.

- Roll 46. Birth Records (3 vols.) 1899-1907
  Revolutionary War Pensions
  Will Records 1831-1859.

Washington County:
- Roll 3. Marriage Record (A) 1815-1828, (B) 1828-1833, (C) 1833-1837, (D) 1837-1844, (E) 1844-1847, (F) 1847-1857, (G) 1858-1867, (H) 1867-1874.

- Roll 4. Marriage Record (I) 1874-1881, (J) 1881-1888
  Birth Record 1882-1888, 1882-1900, 1890-1900, 1896-1901, 1901-1905, 1904-1905, 1905-1907.
  Commissioners Record (A) 1817-1824, (B) 1824-1839.

MICROFILM (Cont'd)

INDIANA (Cont'd)
    Washington County:
        Roll 5.   Commissioners Record (C) 1839-1846
                (D) 1846-1855
                Tract Book: Deed Record (Vol. A) 1814-1817, (Vol. B) 1817-1823, (Vol. C) 1823-1826.

        Roll 6.   Deed Record (Vol. D) 1824-1828, (Vol. E) 1827-1830
                Will Record 1821-1830
                Circuit Court Minute Book 1814-1818
                Probate Order Book (A) 1814-1824, (B) not photographed, (C) 1837-1841.
                Appraisement of Benjamin Parks Estate 1835
                Sale Bill of Benjamin Parks Estate 1835.

KENTUCKY:
    Newspapers:
        Lexington Herald, 1933, 1935

        Lexington Leader 1935

        Louisville Courier-Journal 1930-1931.

LOUISIANA:
    BIRTH RECORDS, STATE BOARD OF HEALTH, 1911-1941.
    State Board of Health, New Orleans, La.

    BIRTH RECORDS, CITY OF NEW ORLEANS, 1847-1901.
    New Orleans Board of Health, New Orleans, La.

NEW JERSEY:    (Filmed by New Jersey Historical Records Survey showing location of original records). Films in possession of American Documentation Institute, Washington, D. C.

    MINUTES OF THE COUNCIL OF PROPRIETORS OF THE EASTERN DIVISION OF NEW JERSEY (ABI), 1685-1705, 32 ft.
    Surveyor General's Office, City Hall, Perth Amboy, N. J.

    MINUTES OF THE COUNCIL OF PROPRIETORS OF THE EASTERN DIVISION OF NEW JERSEY, 1725-64. 36 ft.
    Surveyor General's Office, City Hall, Perth Amboy, N. J.

    MINUTES OF THE COUNCIL OF PROPRIETORS OF THE EASTERN DIVISION OF NEW JERSEY, 1764-94. No. "B" 34 ft.
    Surveyor General's Office, City Hall, Perth Amboy, N. J.

## MICROFILM (Cont'd)

## NEW JERSEY (Cont'd)

MINUTES OF THE COUNCIL OF PROPRIETORS OF THE EASTERN
DIVISION OF NEW JERSEY, 1794-1866, 30 ft.
Surveyor General's Office, City Hall, Perth Amboy, N. J.

MINUTES OF THE SUPREME COURT, 1681-1709   ("The Burlington
Court Book")  20 ft.
Supreme Court Clerk's Office, State House Annex,
Trenton, N. J.

MINUTES OF THE SUPREME COURT, 1760-64.  25 ft.
Supreme Court Clerk's Office, State House Annex,
Trenton, N. J.

MINUTES OF THE SUPREME COURT, 1761-65.  30 ft.
Supreme Court Clerk's Office, State House Annex, Trenton, N. J.

MINUTES OF THE SUPREME COURT, 1767-68.  30 ft.
Supreme Court Clerk's Office, State House Annex, Trenton, N. J.

A BILL IN THE CHANCERY OF NEW JERSEY.  (Hand printed by James
Parker in New York, 1747) 15 ft.

COURT OF COMMON RIGHTS OF CHANCERY, 1684.  (D - 2. LIBER 2).
35 ft.  Secretary of State's Vault, State House, Trenton, N. J.

EARLY INDEX TO BURLINGTON COURT MINUTES, 1681-1709.  27 ft.
Supreme Court Clerk's Vault, State House Annex, Trenton, N. J.

BURLINGTON SUPREME COURT DOCKET, 1731-37.  FEB. TERM.
1 VOLUME.  30 ft.
Supreme Court Clerk's Safe, State House Annex, Trenton, N. J.

BURLINGTON SUPREME COURT DOCKET, MAY TERM 1742.  14 ft.
Supreme Court Clerk's Safe, State House Annex, Trenton, N. J.

LIB A FOR JUDGMENTS, 1755-1758.  10 ft.
Supreme Court Clerk's Office, State House Annex, Trenton, N. J.

MINUTES OF THE COURT OF SESSIONS AND COMMON PLEAS COURT, 1700-1813,
1713-1731, 1730-1739.  30 ft.
Gloucester County Historical Society, Gloucester County Building,
Woodbury, N. J.

SUPREME COURT DOCKET, MAY TERM, 1738 - Nov. 1741, VOL. 2.  30 ft.
Supreme Court Clerk's Safe, State House Annex, Trenton, N. J.

SUPREME COURT DOCKET, MAY TERM. 1742-45.  15 ft.
Supreme Court Clerk's Vault, State House Annex, Trenton, N. J.

## MICROFILM (Cont'd)

### NEW JERSEY (Cont'd)

SUPREME COURT DOCKET, NOVEMBER 1745-48. No. 4. 22 ft.
Supreme Court Clerk's Vault, State House Annex, Trenton, N. J.

MINUTES AND RULES OF THE SUPREME COURT, 1704-15. 10 ft.
Supreme Court Clerk's Vault, State House Annex, Trenton, N. J.

MINUTES AND RULES OF THE SUPREME COURT, 1716-31. 14 ft.
Supreme Court Clerk's Vault, State House Annex, Trenton, N. J.

MINUTES OF THE SUPREME COURT, 1772-76. 5 ft.
Clerk's Office, Supreme Court, State House Annex, Trenton, N. J.

MINUTES OF THE SUPREME COURT, 1775-76. 5 ft.
Clerk's Office, Supreme Court, State House Annex, Trenton, N. J.

SUPREME COURT MINUTES MEMORANDA, 1782-83. 5 ft.
Clerk's Office, Supreme Court, State House Annex, Trenton, N. J.

LIBER AAA OF DEEDS, 1680. 30 ft.
Secretary of State's Vault, State House, Trenton, N. J.

DEEDS - PATENTS, LIBER I, 1666-82. 30 ft.
Secretary of State, State House, Trenton, N. J.

MINUTES OF GLOUCESTER COUNTY FREEHOLDERS, 1700-1812, 2 VOLUMES.
45 ft.
Gloucester County Historical Society, Gloucester County Building,
Woodbury, N. J.

OLD ROAD BOOK, 1745-1775. 30 ft.
County Clerk's Office, County Court House, Somerville, N. J.

BOARD OF CHOSEN FREEHOLDERS OF SOMERSET COUNTY. MINUTES No. 1 -
1772-1810. 25 ft.
Treasurer's Vault, County Clerk House, Somerville, N. J.

MINUTES OF PISCATAWAY TOWNSHIP, FEB. 1, 1682 to JULY 1933. 54 ft.
Township Clerk, Township Hall, New Market, N. J.

WOODBRIDGE TOWNSHIP FREEHOLDERS BOOK, LIBER A, 1668-1757, 28 ft.
Clerk's Vault, Woodbridge City Hall, Woodbridge, N. J.

VOTES & PROCEEDINGS OF THE COMMON COUNCIL OF THE CITY OF
BURLINGTON. 25 ft.
104 Vault - Burlington City Hall, Burlington, N. J.

MICROFILM (Cont'd)

NEW JERSEY (Cont'd)

    CHESTER TOWNSHIP'S "PONSOKING" 1692-1823. 15 ft.
    David L. Lippincott, 1 East Oak Street, Moorestown, N. J.

    BURLINGTON TOWN BOOK, 1693-1780. 30 ft.
    Masonic Home Vault, Masonic Home, Burlington Township, N. J.

    BURLINGTON RECORDS, 1680-1717. 27 ft.
    Secretary of State's Vault, State House, Trenton, N. J.

    ROAD BOOK A. ESSEX COUNTY. 12-3-1698 - 3-30-1804. 30 ft.
    Room 228, County Clerk's Vault, Hall of Records, Newark, N. J.

    COMMISSIONS: ACTS OF ASSEMBLY & C., 1682-1898. 40 ft.
    Secretary of State's Vault (Locker No. 12), State House,
    Trenton, N. J.

    COMMISSIONS A. A. A. 1703-74. 30 ft.
    Secretary of State's Vault, State House, Trenton, N. J.

    DECLARATIONS OF INTENTIONS OF ALIENS, FEB. 1852. 10 ft.
    Supreme Court Clerk's Office, State House Annex, Trenton, N. J.

    RECORDS OF NATURALIZATION - MINORS, 1851. BOOK No. 1. 5 ft.
    Clerk's Office, Supreme Court, State House Annex, Trenton, N. J.

    RECORDS OF NATURALIZATION - MINORS, 1851-73. BOOK NO. 2. 10 ft.
    Clerk's Office, Supreme Court, State House Annex, Trenton, N. J.

    MINUTE BOOK OF GOV. CARTERET, 1665. (DEEDS LIBER 3). 30 ft.
    Secretary of State's Vault (Locker No. 12), State House,
    Trenton, N. J.

    THE STATE VS. CHAS. BOWLSBEY, MAY 14, 1778. 1 ft.
    Surrogate's Office Vault, Hall of Records, Morristown, N. J.

    THE TREASURER OF EASTERN DIVISION OF NEW JERSEY TO THE COMMISSIONER
    OF LOAN OFFICE OF COUNTY OF MORRIS, May 27, 1776 to April 30,
    1838. 10 ft.
    Surrogate's Office Vault, Hall of Records, Morristown, N. J.

    PROCEEDINGS OF JUSTICE AND FREEHOLDERS, COUNTY OF MORRIS, MAY 10,
    1786 to DECEMBER 1, 1823. 10 ft.
    Surrogate's Office Vault, Hall of Records, Morristown, N. J.

    DOCUMENTARY EVIDENCE, OLD KINGS HIGHWAY, 3 VOLUMES. 45 ft.
    Gloucester County Historical Society, Gloucester County Building,
    Woodbury, N. J.

    HISTORIC HOUSES OF WOODBURY, GLOUCESTER COUNTY, 2 VOLUMES. 30 ft.
    Gloucester County, Historical Society, Gloucester County Building,
    Woodbury, N. J.

MICROFILM (Cont'd)

NEW YORK: (Filmed by New York City Historical Records Survey)

    AMERICAN LOYALIST TRANSCRIPTS 1783-1790
    New York Public Library, New York City
    Subject Cards of United States History in New York Public
    Library Card Catalog.

PENNSYLVANIA: (Filmed by New Jersey Historical Records Survey showing location of original records)

    COURT OF COMMON PLEAS OF BUCKS COUNTY, HIRAM H. KELLER, PRES.
    JUDGE, DOYLESTOWN, PENNSYLVANIA.
    Commission on Historical Court Records of the Pennsylvania Bar
    Assn., Philadelphia, Pa.

    MINUTE BOOK - COMMON PLEAS & QUARTER SESSIONS, BUCK COUNTY,
    PENNSYLVANIA, 1684-1730.
    Clerk of Quarter Sessions Office, Bucks County Court House,
    Doylestown, Pa.

    SESSIONS DOCKET, 1715-1753, BUCKS COUNTY, PENNSYLVANIA.
    Clerk of Quarter Sessions Office, Bucks County Court House,
    Doylestown, Pa.

    RULES, FORMS & FEES OF COURT FROM 1770 to 1809, BUCKS COUNTY,
    PENNSYLVANIA.
    Office of Clerk of Quarter Sessions, Bucks County Court House,
    Doylestown, Pa.

# APPENDIX II

## PAPERS AND ARTICLES

Andreassen, John C. L., The Inventory of Manuscript Collections in the South. A paper read at the Fourth Annual Meeting of the southern Historical Association, New Orleans, La., November 3, 1938, 10 p.

----------- ---------- The National Survey of County Archives. A paper read at the Second Annual Convention of the Society of American Archivists, Springfield, Ill., October 26, 1938. Washington, D. C. The Historical Records Survey, December 1938, 12 p.

Binkley, Robert C., The Why of the White Collar Program. Extracts from a paper prepared for a joint meeting of the Society of American Archivists and the American Historical Association, Chicago, Ill., December 1938, 12 p.

----------- ---------- History for a Democracy. Presented as the Annual Address of the 88th Annual Meeting of the Minnesota Historical Society, January 1937. Reprinted from Minnesota History, Vol. 18, No. 1, 1-27 p.

----------- ---------- "The Cultural Program of the WPA" in Harvard Educational Review. Vol. 9, No. 2, March 1939, 156-174 p. Also reprinted separately.

Child, Sargent B., Status and Plans for Completion of the Inventories of the Historical Records Survey. A paper read at the Joint Program Committee on Archives and Libraries of the American Library Association, The Conference of Historical Societies, the Midwest Members of the Society of American Archivists and the Historical Records Survey, May 27, 1940, 12 p.; Also in Archives and Libraries, Chicago, Ill., 1940, 12-25 p.

----------- ---------- What is Past is Prologue.--- The Historical Records Survey. A Report read at the Annual Meeting of the American Library Association, Milwaukee, Wis., June 23, 1942, 23 p.; Also contains Final Report of the American Imprints Inventory by Don Farran; Reprinted without the Final Report of the American Imprints Inventory in The American Archivist, Vol. V, No. 4, October 1942, 217-227 p.

Eliot, Margaret S., "Inventories and Guides to Historical Manuscript Collections" in Archives and Libraries, American Library Association Chicago, Ill., 1940, 26-35 p.

----------- ---------- "The Manuscript Program of the Historical Records Survey" in Public Documents with Archives and Libraries, American Library Association, Chicago, Ill., 1938, 317-326 p.

## PAPERS AND ARTICLES (Cont'd)

Evans, Luther H., "The Historical Records Survey" in Public Documents, American Historical Association, Chicago, Ill., 1936, 209-214 p.

----- ---------- Next Step in the Improvement of Local Archives. An address delivered before the National Association of State Libraries, 40th Annual Convention, New York City, June 21-25, 1937. 6p; Also in Public Documents, American Library Association, Chicago, Ill., 1937, 276-285 p.

----- ---------- "Archives as Materials for the Teaching of History." An article based upon an address delivered at the 19th Annual Indiana History Conference, Indianapolis, Ind., December 11, 1937, in Indiana Historical Bulletin Vol. 15, No. 2, 136-163 p.

----- ---------- Government and Local History. An address delivered at a conference on State and local history held in connection with the Annual Meeting of the Pacific Coast Branch of the American Historical Association, Stanford University, California, December 28, 1938. Reprinted from The Pacific Historical Review Vol. VIII No. 1, March 1939, 97-104 p.

----- ---------- "The Local Archives Program of the WPA Historical Records Survey" in Public Documents with Archives and Libraries, American Library Association, Chicago, Ill. 1938, 284-300 p.

----- ---------- WPA Fashions New Tools for Research. Presented before the 31st Annual Meeting of the Mississippi Valley Historical Association, Indianapolis, Ind., April 28, 1938, 16 p.       39-26192

----- ---------- The Historical Records Survey. A Statement on its Progress and Accomplishments Presented to the Sub-Committee of the Senate Committee on Education and Labor, in connection with the Bill to Create a Permanent Bureau of Fine Arts, March 1, 1938, 18 p.       38-26503

----- ---------- The Historical Records Survey and its Progress in New England. Prepared for the New England Conference of Librarians, Portsmouth, N. H. June 21, 1939, 18 p.

----- ---------- Preservation of the Nation's Records. Presented before the 48th Continental Congress, National Society of the Daughters of the American Revolution, April 19, 1939, 12 p.

Evans, Luther H. and Weiner, Edyth W. "The Analysis of County Records" in The American Archivist Vol. I, No. 4, October 1938, 186-200 p.

Hamer, Philip M. "Federal Archives outside of the District of Columbia" in Proceedings of the Society of American Archivists, Washington, D. C. June 18-19, 1937. 83-89 p.

## PAPERS AND ARTICLES (Cont'd)

"Report of the National Director of the Survey of Federal Archives to the Work Progress Administration" in Second Annual Report of the Archivist of the United States. 1936, 88-103 p.

"Report of the National Director of the Survey of Federal Archives to the Work Progress Administration for the Fiscal Year ending June 30, 1937" in Third Annual Report of the Archivist of the United States, 1937, 93-110 p.

"Report of the Work of the Survey of Federal Archives for the Fiscal Year ending June 30, 1938, by the Associate National Director of the Historical Records Survey in charge of the Inventory of Federal Archives in the States" in Fourth Annual Report of the Archivist of the United States, 1938, 62-64 p.

"Report of the Work of the Survey of Federal Archives for the Fiscal Year ending June 30, 1939 by the Associate National Director of the Historical Records Survey in charge of the Inventory of Federal Archives in the States" in Fifth Annual Report of the Archivist of the United States, 1939, 89-91 p.

"Report of the Work of the Survey of Federal Archives for the Fiscal Year ending June 30, 1940" in Sixth Annual Report of the Archivist of the United States, 1940, 91-93 p.

"Report of the Work of the Survey of Federal Archives for the Fiscal Year ending June 30, 1941 by the Assistant Director of the Historical Records Survey" in Seventh Annual Report of the Archivist of the United States, 1941, 89-91 p.

"Report of the Work of the Survey of Federal Archives for the Fiscal Year ending June 30, 1942 by the Assistant Director of the Historical Records Survey Projects in charge of the Inventory of Federal Archives in the States" in Eighth Annual Report of the Archivist of the United States, 1941-42, page 82.

Hogan, William R. The Historical Records Survey -- An Outside View. Read at the 3rd Annual Meeting of the Society of American Archivists, October 13, 1939, 17 p.

Kellar, Herbert A. "An Appraisal of the Historical Records Survey" in Archives and Libraries, American Library Association, Chicago, Ill., 1940, 44-59 p.

Lacy, Dan., The Historical Records Survey and the Librarian. A paper read before the Archives and Libraries Section of the American Library Association, Boston, Mass., June 21, 1941, 19 p.

———— ———————— Administrative History in Relation to State Archives. A Paper read before the Annual Meeting of the Society of American Archivists, Montgomery, Ala., Nov. 11, 1940, 8 p.

## PAPERS AND ARTICLES (Cont'd)

MacFarland, George M., "Archives and Local Administrative History" in The American Archivist Vol. III, No. 3, July 1941, 170-177 p.

McMurtrie, Douglas C., The Record of American Imprints. Extract from the Proceedings of the Conference of State and Local Historical Societies Held at the Historical Society of Pennsylvania, December 31, 1937, 5 p.

McMurtrie, Douglas C., "A Nationwide Inventory of American Imprints under WPA Auspices." in Public Documents, American Library Association, Chicago, Ill., 1938, 301-316 p.; Reprinted separately, Chicago, Ill., 1938, 23 p.

---------- ------------ "Further Progress in the Record of American Printing" in Archives and Libraries, American Library Association, Chicago, Ill., 1940, 36-43 p.; Reprinted separately, Chicago, Ill., 1940, 12 p.

Miller, George J., "Contributions to New Jersey History" in The Genealogical Magazine of New Jersey Vol. XI, No. 2, 25-31 p.

Rifkind, Herbert R., The Historical Records Survey and the Political Scientist, Chicago, Ill., 1940, 16 p.

Roach, George W., "Final Report, The Historical Records Survey in Upstate New York, 1936-1942" reprinted from New York History, January 1943.

Scammell, J. Marius, Librarians and Archives. Reprinted from The Library Quarterly Vol. IX, No. 4, October 1939, 432-444 p.

---------- ----------- Historical Records Survey, Progress Report, 1938-39, in Archives and Libraries, American Library Association, Chicago, Ill. 1939, p. 11-21.

Stephenson, Jean and Woodward, Ellen S., "Rediscovering the Nation's Records" in Daughters American Revolution Magazine, October 1936, 4 p.

APPENDIX III

## MANUALS

Manual of the Survey of Historical Records (with attached forms) (16 p. mimeo., January 1936)

Supplement No. 1.  Cooperation with Private Organizations. (1 p. mimeo., 1936)

Supplement No. 3.  Church Records Form. (4 p. mimeo., 1936)

Supplement No. 4.  Instructions for Editing Guides to Public Records. (19 p. mimeo., 1936)

Supplement No. 5.  Further Instructions for Editing Guides to Public Records. (13 p. mimeo., January 1937)

Supplement No. 6.  The Preparation of Guides to Manuscripts. (22 p. mimeo., September 1937)

Supplement No. 7.  Instructions for use of WPA Form 12-13 Revised. 6 p. mimeo., October 1937)

Supplement No. 8.  Instructions for the Preparation of Individual Manuscripts Form, WPA Form 19HR. (6 p. mimeo., 1937)

Editing of Public Records Inventories. Memorandum issued to Assistant State Supervisors, Historical Records Survey (7 p. mimeo., June 12, 1936)

Instructions for the Preparation of Inventories of Public Records by the Historical Records Survey Projects. WPA Technical Series, Research and Records Projects Circular No. 5, Vol. 1, (132 p. mimeo., May 1941)   40-29084

The Form and Use of Footnotes and Bibliography in the Publications of the Historical Records Survey. WPA Technical Series, Research and Records Projects Circular No. 4. (18 p. mimeo., September 1940)

Preparation of Inventories of Manuscripts. A Circular of Instructions for the Use of the Historical Records Survey. (iv, 58 p. mimeo., October 1940)

Preliminary Instructions on the Preparation of Inventories of Church Archives. (17 p. mimeo., March 1938)

The Manual of the Survey of Federal Archives. (29 p. mimeo., February 1936)

## MANUALS (Cont'd)

American Imprints Inventory; Manual of Procedure:
    1st Edition (35 p. mimeo., June 1938)                        38-26759

    2nd Edition. (44 p. mimeo., August 1938)                38-28888

    3rd Edition. (45 p. mimeo., October 1938)               38-26982

    4th Edition. (48 p. mimeo., January 1939)               39-26343

    5th Edition. (48 p. mimeo., April 1939)                40-26222

Instructions for Examination of Newspaper Files for Materials Relating to the History of the Press. (12 p. mimeo., 1937)      39-26662

Instructions for the Description of Broadsides:
    1st Edition. (16 p. mimeo., January 1939)               39-26263

Manual for Newspaper Transcription. (Prepared by the Pennsylvania Historical Survey. 29 p. mimeo., 1941)      41-26012

Collection of Information Concerning Vital Statistics Records by the Historical Records Survey Projects. Professional and Service Letter No. 75. (7 p. mimeo., September 3, 1940)

Instructions to Field Workers for Briefing Historical and Legal Material in County Records with work samples. (Prepared by the Illinois Historical Records Survey. 16 p. mimeo., May 1938)

APPENDIX IV

## REPORTS AND SUMMARIES

The Historical Records Survey in New Jersey: Description of its Purpose, Account of its Accomplishments, Bibliography of its Publications. (66 p. mimeo., 1941)

Comments on the Michigan Historical Records Survey. (limited edition) (70 p. mimeo., January 1942)

Comments on the Missouri Historical Records Survey. (iv, 27 p. mimeo., 1941)

Services and Accomplishments of the Missouri Historical Records Survey. (iv, 12 p. mimeo., 1941)

Missouri Historical Records Survey: Annual Report, 1941. (18 p. mimeo., January 1942)

Report on the Accomplishments and Activities of the Oklahoma Historical Records Survey, February 1936 - January 1940. (15 p. mimeo., 1940)                40-26469

Final Report and Inventory of the Vermont Historical Records Survey. (ii, 73 p. mimeo., June 1942)                42-25624

A Report of the Work, Accomplishments, Services and Status of the Missouri Historical Records Survey as of April 7, 1942.

Report on the Louisiana Statewide Records Project and the Historical Records Survey. (22 p. mimeo., May 1940)

Report on the Status of the Statewide Records Project, ... and the Survey of Federal Archives, Louisiana. (22 p. mimeo., October 1941.)

## MISCELLANEOUS

Distribution of Publications of the Historical Records Survey Projects.
Professional and Service Letter No. 63. (13 p. mimeo., May 1940)

Professional and Service Letter No. 63, Revised. (18 p. mimeo., Dec. 1940)

Mailing List for Church Publications (Memorandum to State Directors of Historical Records Survey from Luther H. Evans. (6 p. mimeo., July 17, 1939)

## MISCELLANEOUS (Cont'd)

Amendment to Special Church Mailing List (7 p. mimeo., June 14, 1940)

List of Publications, Historical Records Survey, Work Projects Administration. (17 p. mimeo., December 1939)

Check List of Historical Records Survey Publications, Work Projects Administration. (38 p. mimeo., September 12, 1940)

Supplement to Check List of Historical Records Survey Publications issued September 12, 1940. (10 p. mimeo., December 23, 1940)

List of Publications Historical Records Survey, WPA., (including those approved for publication). (69 p. mimeo., September 1941)

List of Mimeographed Volumes of the Inventory of Federal Archives in the States Completed by February 29, 1940. (6 p. offset, 1940)

## APPENDIX V

### *DEPOSITORIES OF UNPUBLISHED MATERIAL

**ALABAMA:**
Department of Archives & History, Montgomery, Ala.

**ARIZONA:**
Arizona State Department of Library & Archives, Phoenix, Ariz.

**ARKANSAS:**
University of Arkansas Library, Fayetteville, Ark.

**CALIFORNIA:**
State Archives, Sacramento, Calif. (No. Calif. materials.)
Los Angeles County Museum, Los Angeles, Calif. (So. Calif. materials.)

**COLORADO:**
State Historical Society, Denver, Colo.

**CONNECTICUT:**
State Library, Hartford, Conn.

**FLORIDA:**
Dept. of Archives, Tallahassee, Fla.

**DELAWARE:**
Department of Archives, State University, Dover, Del.

**GEORGIA:**
University of Georgia, Athens, Ga.

**IDAHO:**
Secretary of State, Boise, Idaho.

**ILLINOIS:**
University of Illinois. (Lincolniana.)
State Historical Library. (Inventories of manuscript collections.)
State Archives. (All other materials.)

**IOWA:**
State Department of History & Archives, Des Moines, Iowa.

**INDIANA:**
Indiana State Library, Indianapolis, Ind.

**KANSAS:**
Kansas State Historical Society, Topeka, Kans.

---

* Where one depository only is listed, that depository has custody of all unpublished material for that state. Exceptions are indicated where a specific type of material is shown in parenthesis immediately following the name of a depository.

## DEPOSITORIES OF UNPUBLISHED MATERIAL (Cont'd)

KENTUCKY:
    University of Kentucky Library, Lexington, Ky.

LOUISIANA:
    Department of Archives & History, Louisiana State University, Baton Rouge, La.

MAINE:
    Work Projects Administration warehouse, Portland, Me.

MASSACHUSETTS:
    Forbes Library, Northampton, Mass.

MARYLAND:
    Hall of Records, Annapolis, Md.

MICHIGAN:
    Michigan Historical Collection, University of Michigan, Ann Arbor, Mich.

MINNESOTA:
    State Historical Society, St. Paul, Minn.

MISSISSIPPI:
    Department of Archives & History, Jackson, Miss.

MISSOURI:
    University of Missouri, Columbia, Mo.

MONTANA:
    State College, Bozeman, Mont.

NEBRASKA:
    State Historical Society, Lincoln, Nebr.

NEVADA:
    Nevada Historical Society, Reno, Nev.

NEW HAMPSHIRE:
    University of New Hampshire, Manchester, N. H.

NEW JERSEY:
    Columbia University Library, New York, N. Y. (Atlas of Congressional Roll Calls.) (Presidential Messages, Papers & Executive Orders.)
    State Library, Trenton, N. J. (All other materials.)

NEW MEXICO:
    State Museum, Santa Fe, New Mexico

DEPOSITORIES OF UNPUBLISHED MATERIAL (Cont'd)

NEW YORK CITY:
    New York City Historical Society. (List and index of Early American Portrait Painters.) (American Slavery imprints.)
    Columbia University Library. (George D. White Papers.)
    Cooper Union for the Advancement of Society & Art. (Calendar of Cooper-Hewitt Papers.)
    American-Jewish Historical Society. (Directory of Jewish Congregations (United States of America).) ("America in Yiddish Literature".) (Yiddish Anthology.)
    Modern Art Film Library. (Film Index.)
    New York Public Library. ("Negroes of New York.")
    New York City Department of Health, Division of Vital Statistics. (Public Vital Statistics.)
    Municipal Reference Library. (All other materials.)

NEW YORK STATE:
    State Library, Albany, N. Y.

NORTH CAROLINA:
    Historical Commission, Raleigh, N. C.

NORTH DAKOTA:
    State Library Commission, Bismark, So. Dak.

OHIO:
    Western Reserve Historical Society, Cleveland, Ohio (Historic sites material.)
    Hayes Memorial Library, Fremont, Ohio. (Bibliographical material.)
    Ohio State Archaeological & Historical Society, Columbus, Ohio. (All other materials.)

OKLAHOMA:
    State Library, Oklahoma City, Okla.

OREGON:
    Department of History, University of Oregon, Eugene, Oregon.

PENNSYLVANIA:
    Historical Commission, Harrisburg, Penn.

RHODE ISLAND:
    State Library, Providence, R. I.

SOUTH DAKOTA:
    University of South Dakota, Vermillion, So. Dak.

TENNESSEE:
    State Planning Commission, Nashville, Tenn.

TEXAS:
    University of Texas, Austin, Tex.

DEPOSITORIES OF UNPUBLISHED MATERIAL (Cont'd)

UTAH:
    State Historical Society, Salt Lake City, Utah.

VERMONT:
    State Historical Society, Montpelier, Vt.

VIRGINIA:
    Baptist Historical Society, University of Richmond, Richmond, Va.
        (Church Archives.)
    State Library, Richmond, Va. (All other materials.)

WEST VIRGINIA:
    Department of Archives & History, Charleston, W. Va.
        (Historical Materials.)
    West Virginia University Library, Morgantown, W. Va.
        (All other materials.)

WASHINGTON:
    State College, Pullman, Wash.

WYOMING:
    State Library, Cheyenne, Wyo.

WISCONSIN:
    State Historical Society, Madison, Wis.

DISTRICT OF COLUMBIA:
    Library of Congress.